# GODS OF GRINDHOUSE

## Interviews with Exploitation Filmmakers

Edited by Andrew J. Rausch

*Foreword* by Christopher Wayne Curry

*Introduction* by Chris Watson

# Gods of Grindhouse:
# Interviews with Exploitation Filmmakers

© 2013 Andrew J. Rausch
All rights reserved.

No portion of this publication may be reproduced, stored, and/or copied electronically (except for academic use as a source), nor transmitted in any form or by any means without the prior written permission of the publisher and/or author.

Published in the USA by:
BearManor Media
P.O. Box 1129
Duncan, OK 73534-1129
www.BearManorMedia.com

ISBN:    1-59393-734-2
ISBN-13: 978-1-59393-734-8

Printed in the United States

Design and Layout by Scot Penslar

Front cover artwork by R.D. Riley

Photographs courtesy of Christoper Wayne Curry and ED Tucker

# Table of Contents

**Foreword** *by Christopher Wayne Curry* . . . . . . . . . . . . . . . . . 3
**Introduction** *by Chris Watson* . . . . . . . . . . . . . . . . . . . . . . . 5
**Preface** . . . . . . . . . . . . . . . . . . . . . . . . . . . . . . . . . . . . . . . . 9
**Charles Band** *by Bryan Layne* . . . . . . . . . . . . . . . . . . . . . . . 11
**Greydon Clark** *by Mike White* . . . . . . . . . . . . . . . . . . . . . . 19
**Larry Cohen** *by Andrew J. Rausch* . . . . . . . . . . . . . . . . . . . 25
**Roger Corman** *by Andrew J. Rausch* . . . . . . . . . . . . . . . . . 35
**David F. Friedman** *by Nathaniel Thompson* . . . . . . . . . . . . 43
**Frank Henenlotter** *by Colleen Wanglund* . . . . . . . . . . . . . . 55
**Jack Hill** *by Chris Watson* . . . . . . . . . . . . . . . . . . . . . . . . . 65
**Alejandro Jodorowsky** *by Andrew Leavold* . . . . . . . . . . . . 73
**Lloyd Kaufman** *by David Carroll and Kyla Ward* . . . . . . . . 79
**Herschell Gordon Lewis** *by Andrew J. Rausch* . . . . . . . . . . 89
**William Lustig** *by Devin Faraci* . . . . . . . . . . . . . . . . . . . . . 95
**Russ Meyer** *by Sandra Gin Yep and Mike Carroll* . . . . . . . . 101
**Ted V. Mikels** *by Andrew Leavold* . . . . . . . . . . . . . . . . . . . 109
**Bill Rebane** *by ED Tucker* . . . . . . . . . . . . . . . . . . . . . . . . . 121
**John A. Russo** *by Andrew J. Rausch* . . . . . . . . . . . . . . . . . 141
**Ray Dennis Steckler** *by ED Tucker* . . . . . . . . . . . . . . . . . . 149
**Acknowledgments** . . . . . . . . . . . . . . . . . . . . . . . . . . . . . . 163
**Index** . . . . . . . . . . . . . . . . . . . . . . . . . . . . . . . . . . . . . . . . . 165

# Foreword
## by Christopher Wayne Curry

In 2006, when the Quentin Tarantino/Robert Rodriguez faux drive-in double feature *Grindhouse* tanked at the box office, the consensus was that interest in this type of product had reached its pinnacle, and its end. In keeping with the true spirit of things, *Grindhouse* should have done poorly. It was sending up a form of cinema that lived (and died) largely upon its ability to lure patrons in on promises that simply could not be kept. Still, that's only a small portion of the story, and the kicker is that *Grindhouse* did deliver the goods.

Fortunately, the crystal ball can be cloudy and the grindhouse juggernaut forges on. Cinephiles, of dubious tastes, apparently still love to experience films that exercise language, culture, customs, fashions, and ideologies from a bygone era, thus making themselves a cross-section of humanity that snubs its collective noses at the Hollywood norm. A cross section of humanity to be thankful for, to be sure.

The first legitimate blip on the radar that grindhouse cinema had a place in filmic culture came in 1986 with the publication of *Incredibly Strange Films*. Here a gaggle of counter-culture writers, artists, musicians, observers, and general devotees of the weird interviewed the likes of Russ Meyer, H.G. Lewis, Larry Cohen, and Ted V. Mikels. Teen juvenile delinquent, biker, and industrial films were also dissected, but the book's primary focus was on the grindhouse auteurs, and what a book it was.

For years to come, *Incredibly Strange Films* would be seen as the bible of underground, under-examined, and under-appreciated cinema. The directors investigated within those pages had been enlisted to provide a cinematic escape route to a runaway world of sex, violence, gore, and the all-around bizarre.

Transport to 2013, and prolific author Andrew J. Rausch has gathered an altogether different gaggle of misfit movie enthusiasts to help punctuate the fact that grindhouse cinema has seemingly taken on a life of its own. A mutant life perhaps, but a life of its own just the same (applicable books, magazines, websites, all-night film retrospectives, and conventions abound).

Further proof is evident in the fact that numerous other grindhouse-type films have emerged as of late. Give *Machete* a day in court, or perhaps *Hobo with a Shotgun*. Maybe *Hellride*, *The Devil's Rejects*, or *Black Dynamite* are more appealing. Even mainstream Hollywood tossed in a play with *Black Snake Moan*. It didn't work, but Hollywood has been missing the mark for years.

In short, that's what this book is — a celebration of anti-Hollywood films, made by outside Hollywood directors for fans of film without Hollywood pretension and its sense of shine, sheen, morals, and censorship.

**Christopher Wayne Curry** is the author of the books *A Taste of Blood: The Films of Herschell Gordon Lewis* and *Film Alchemy: The Independent Cinema of Ted V. Mikels*.

# Introduction
## by Chris Watson

I set up an interview with Jack Hill, taking him up on meeting for a lunch that would take place in cult movie heaven. The restaurant was hidden away in an area between Los Angeles and my home in Encino. I looked for and found a place to sit down to soak up the architectural beauty. My eyes trailed down to the people as I tried to soak in the atmosphere. They were a mixture of arty and upper class types. My eyes zeroed in on Herb Jefferson, Jr. sitting alone at a table; I had seen Herb at numerous conventions with similar results. I debated talking to Herb as Jack Hill arrived. Jack was older and friendly; he was not the guy you envision being responsible for classic, violent blaxploitation films. Instead, Jack looks like your uncle who finds yoga all the rage.

I joined Jack and his wife in the back of the restaurant, pulling out my bloodstained Sony VX2000 to record the interview. As I set the camera upon the table, my face reddened. I expected a large camera and questions about blaxploitation to draw interest. Wouldn't people be curious who was getting interviewed? Wouldn't the questions pique interest? No one around gave us a second look. At the time, I assumed people were just used to seeing interviews conducted.

The interview began with Jack talking about a white actor who worked on one of his films. In the 1970s, Jack ran into the actor who would talk about being embarrassed by the films. Then, 20 years later, Jack saw the same actor at a convention charging $20 for a photo from those films. This is the stigma that is often attached to cult or grindhouse films; the actors are embarrassed by them. A lot of times the actors don't even know the films have a following. I interviewed an actress recently who didn't know one of her films — from 20 years ago — had even been released. Grindhouse films often run under the radar and are forgotten until they build an audience.

The interview continued and a lot of the questions got normal, conditioned responses. Underlying his responses was a reality; Jack seemed to have interest in other types of films. He was more interested in making films that would be considered for Academy Awards. I was sitting across from a man that many consider a legend, and he wasn't interested in revisiting the type of film that garnered his only drops of fame. Jack showed no interest in making the movies that brought me to this restaurant. Jack was proud of what he'd done, but he didn't see what people like me saw.

The interview ended and Jack walked ahead with no one giving him a second look. I made it to the sidewalk with Jack with about 10 feet ahead of me. He walked within a foot of a small table. At that table were Mick Garris and Shawnee Smith. Garris knows his movies, but he didn't take notice of a legend walking by. As I interviewed more people involved in the blaxploitation world, I noticed it over and over again; they walk among us unnoticed. I've seen the father from *My Big Fat Greek Wedding* get mobbed, but legends of grindhouse cinema can walk among film geeks without a second glance. Grindhouse filmmakers have their small, niche followings, but otherwise go unrecognized in the cinematic world.

There is a stigma to grindhouse films. A lot of the grindhouse filmmakers may be happy with going unrecognized. I was at a convention in Cleveland to record a commentary track for a project featuring Lloyd Kaufman. Lloyd was always helpful and offered to give us some time to be a part of the commentary track. As Lloyd entered the hotel elevator, he noticed actor Robert Z'Dar of *Maniac Cop* fame. Lloyd tried to strike up a friendly conversation. Standing next to Robert was a "filmmaker" named Johnny who drunkenly announced to Lloyd, "Your movies suck!" Lloyd would handle it with class, talking later about similar incidents. Grindhouse filmmakers alienate as many, if not more, audience members as they garner. Audiences are not always accepting of the low budgets and the crazy ploys that come with grindhouse films.

While some people are alienated, others just don't have a clue that these films exist. The first book I participated in was *Reflections on Blaxploitation: Actors and Directors Speak*. The book looked great and I was very proud to have been a part of it, so I tried telling everyone about it. The majority of the time I got asked, "What's that 'B' word?" I discovered that the majority of the world has no clue what the blaxploitation genre is.

The importance of this book is simple; *Gods of Grindhouse* records a part of cinematic history. Grindhouse films are known more today for the Robert Rodriguez/Quentin Tarantino team-up *Grindhouse*. The average person has built their reality around that film, missing out on the grimy theater, the chair with springs sticking out, and other aspects of a theater on the verge of closing. The movies have budget restraints that add to the entertainment because the filmmakers were forced to a new level of creativity; some are entertaining by failing, and others, like Hill, earn a lifetime of respect.

The atmosphere of a grindhouse theater was like no other. One example can be seen in a story a projectionist told me about *Boss Nigger* playing in Los Angeles. The projectionist had to have a security detail. The all African-American crowd threw anything they could find at them as they passed. The crowd was wild, raucous, and unforgettable. The audience would take this vibe into the theater, yelling and throwing things at the screen. The projectionist was still describing the scene 35 years later.

Likewise, grindhouse audience members relish in nostalgic cinematic experiences unlike any other. Grindhouse movies had originality to them. Often, the movies had one or two memorable scenes. Jamaa Fanaka's *Welcome Home Brother Charles* is a perfect example. Most of the movie is low budget with little action until the movie goes into overdrive due to a shocking death-by-penis scene. The movie becomes something that people are still talking about today. Without that scene, is anyone talking about it? The originality made these movies legendary. The grindhouse era was before VHS. There was the constant threat of never seeing these movies again. Many of the films became folklore; you would hear about them but never get the chance to see them. The movies relied on their originality to stand apart from the mainstream studio fare.

Ironically, the markets that killed grindhouse theaters also brought the movies into the mainstream. Grindhouse theaters were often one-screen theaters that barely hung on, showing cheap movies that were four-walled across the country. As VHS and cable came into prominence, the audience disappeared. Grindhouse theaters began closing down, but the movies were slowly released on VHS, cable, DVD, and now through instant viewing. Gone are the days of the beat-up theaters showing movies that you could talk about for the next 30 years. The movies have been brought into the mainstream, killing a generation's movie going experience.

*Gods of Grindhouse* serves two major purposes. First, the book brings back parts of that experience — we get a front row seat to what grindhouse movies were for the audience and the people responsible. Second, the reader gets a full-on education and access to behind-the-scenes stories. We may never get the opportunity to see these movies like those before us, but we can try to relive the experience that these films brought.

**Chris Watson** is a screenwriter and director whose credits include *Zombiegeddon, Evil Ever After,* and *Dahmer vs. Gacy*. He is also the co-author of the books *Reflections on Blaxploitation, Joe Estevez: Wiping Off the Sheen,* and *Dwarfsploitation*.

# Preface

This book is an anthology of interviews conducted at different periods by different writers. Because of this, the interviews within this book are structured differently and have different lengths. Some of them have introductions and some do not. In places where either there is no introduction to an interview or an introduction gives very little background information on the interview subject, a note from the editor has been added.

# Charles Band
## by Bryan Layne

**EDITOR'S NOTE:** Charles Band, the son of director Albert Band, established Full Moon Pictures in the mid-Eighties. Between his work as producer, director, and distributor, Band is responsible for nearly 300 films. As a director he is best known for such films as *Trancers*, *Prehysteria!*, and *Dollman vs. Demonic Toys*. His production credits include such notable titles as *Ghoulies*, *Re-Animator*, *Troll*, and the *Puppet Master* franchise.

Charles Band has been around films his entire life. His father, Albert Band, made films continuously throughout the sixties and seventies. His brother, Richard Band, has been a film composer for decades, writing one of my own personal favorite main title themes for *Re-Animator*.

Charles has close to 300 films under his belt and was one of the first entertainment personalities to exploit the future of cable television and the video market. Just before he started his tour across America for his third annual Full Moon Road Show, Mr. Band was kind enough to talk about his past and the future of Full Moon in general.

***You are still personally appearing at the Full Moon Road Shows?***
Oh, yeah. I skipped it last year, but I am back with it this year. It's going to be very well attended. We got some great venues and a lot of wonderful celebrities. It's going to be a whole lot of fun.

***What brought the idea of the road show about and what was your goal with the whole concept?***
I don't know how or why it all started. It's just that for years I've been making these movies and there have been so many generations that have

seen these films that I felt the whole body of work had taken on a life of its own. In the last two or three years I've attended some conventions. As I got up there and tried to entertain people, I found out that I had some kind of a gift for doing entertaining stuff on stage. Not just talking about my movies, but doing things with audience participation and girls who take their tops off . . . Who knows what kind of crazy things I'll be bringing to the stage. Then I thought that I'm kind of lucky and unique in the sense that I've made so many films in the genre. We would get up on stage at these conventions and have so much fun that the idea of doing a tour entered my mind. You know, much like a rock 'n roll band gets out there and does a tour, performs and tries to spread the word. I'm kind of doing the same thing.

I'm also very, very independent and not affiliated with any studio. I felt it was really hard to get these films out there. We do have reasonable distribution, but it's not like the old days when there were tens of thousands of little "mom and pop" video stores out there that carry independent products. Now, there's a handful of big chains that really don't carry library. They just sort of carry the current releases. The whole dream of having a delivery system over the Internet is great, but not quite here yet. The biggest complaint we always get is fans not being able to find our movies anymore. They can get the newer ones, but they seem to also be interested in the films we did in the 70s and 80s.

So, I thought maybe I should just get on the road and do a tour. That was, sort of, the concept behind the very first tour and it was successful on a lot of levels. We actually didn't make any money; that was a bummer, but we did have thousands of people that showed up, a lot of goodwill and I learned a lot by getting out there and talking to the fans. I started to think I could do all of this again. I'd learned some tricks and I did a second year. I would do around twenty

cities each year, which over thirty days was kind of tough, but the show we put together was great. Now, we have so many things happening with Full Moon and some other new deals we are involved in, that I secured a great promoter who has suggested that less is more. So, instead of trying to do twenty cities, we decided on doing twelve. We also planned the shows for over the weekends, which is really when people are more available.

The idea is, let's get bigger venues and just make these twelve cities a huge success. We booked kind of interesting and strange selections of cities. We're not doing anything very west coast. We're starting off in Phoenix, Arizona and working our way around the country. We're going through the south and for the very first time, I'm bringing the show to New York, right on Times Square. I got a lot of people showing up who are going to… I was just with Bill Shatner yesterday on the set of *Boston Legal* and he's going to make one of the dates because we've done some stuff together. It's kind of a weird little, demented Ozzfest. I'm not exactly sure how I want to describe the road show, but ultimately, I hope it promotes goodwill, our film titles and the fact that some really cool new things are about to happen for Full Moon after being, sort of, a well-kept secret for so many years.

**How about that son of yours? He's had quite the success with a rock music career.**

He has had an amazing success, at a very young age, with the rock band The Calling, they broke up, of course. He's now been in the studio for quite some time and he's releasing, a little later this year, his first solo work. I think his solo stuff is astonishing. Aside of the fact that I'm his father, I can certainly say that some of the songs are really, really powerful and I think he's got some big hits in there. He has always been a musical guy and a singer/songwriter, so the fact that he's actually in this substantially horrible business and already had a big success with a number one song, is just exceptional. He grew up on our movie sets, so he was certainly around the entertainment field. My brother has been a composer his whole life, so my son was surrounded by that, as well. He's very gifted in his own right. He's a relatively small guy, but he's got this very deep voice; a voice that almost doesn't go with his size and stature.

**What can you tell me about hanging out with your father, Albert Band, while on his movie sets as a young boy?**

There's so many phenomenal stories to tell there, that I really don't even know where to begin. I grew up in Italy where my dad made his movies, as well as Spain and Yugoslavia, all the way through the sixties and early seventies. The pictures were either spaghetti westerns or big sword and sand movies. Those were the films he was making back in the day and it was also the beginning of what people now refer to as the spaghetti westerns. You know, these really different and edgier westerns, many which were populated by American stars or American names from television. I was on every one of dad's sets over the years and I was extremely lucky to have been a part of that.

One thing I remember was we were all in Spain making a movie that my dad was producing called, *A Minute to Pray, A Second to Die* and it starred Robert Ryan and Joseph Cotton. These were older American actors, who had bigger successes when they were younger, but they had name value and you really needed that for these movies. So, we had that crew working for us and just outside of Madrid, at a hotel, there was another film crew. It was an all Italian film crew that was making a western that was a lot smaller than ours with this young, almost completely unknown actor who'd only been on American television. That crew turned out to be Sergio Leone's and they were filming a movie called *A Fistful of Dollars*. I remember that the vibes were one that we were the bigger, more expensive American film. It was still a European co-production, but we had three or four of these well-known names attached and then there was this strange, little Italian dude making whatever little Italian western that seemed pretty funny and silly with Clint Eastwood which nobody was really familiar with. But, the rest is, of course, history. *A Minute to Pray, A Second to Die* actually did do quite well and was well acknowledged at the time, but *A Fistful of Dollars* became an institution.

Another time, I think it was around 1978, I was probably three or four films into my career. I was lucky enough, at the time, to be working with some amazing talent who were young and just starting off, like myself. My first movie was a strange little horror film called *Mansion of the Doomed*. It starred Lance Henriksen, Gloria Graham and a few others that were kind of well known at the time. I believe that one was Lance's first movie. My director of photography was Andrew Davis, who became a big Hollywood director that made pictures like *The Fugitive*. My effects guy was Stan Winston who went on to win, I think, five Academy Awards. My editor, who used a pseudonym, was John Carpenter and he actually edited a few of my films. It was one of those great moments in time.

A couple of years later, I was making a movie on location in the suburbs of the Hollywood Hills, a picture called *Tourist Trap* with Chuck Connors. I was sharing the same distributor as John known as Compass. John was making a film called *The Babysitter Murders*. We were literally a block apart on one of these little tree-shaded Hollywood streets. I'm making the bigger movie because I had the big star. John was making *The Babysitter Murders* with a bunch of unknown actors. One day, John and I decided we should visit each others' sets. He walked over to mine and met Chuck. Then I went over to his and saw his steadicam whipping around the house for some of the shots for what would later become known as Halloween. Once again, Tourist Trap has its little niche in the beginning because it is kind of a cool little film, but Halloween became...HALLOWEEN. So, there's a little repeat of history in there somewhere.

A scene from the Charles Band produced film, Re-Animator.

**You've always been independent and done everything yourself. How do you feel about conducting business with major studios?**

It's another business altogether. Big pictures are made by committee and, of course, if you are Steven Spielberg you're really, really having a great time. You truly would have the final word about your film. Few people have that control when it comes to the big studios. I have a lot of friends who are making mainstream films and occasionally I'll visit the set. We'll hang out and I'll hear the good, the bad and the ugly.

The good is when a big project is finally rolling, there's no end of money. It still doesn't change the fact that if the script sucks, you've got nothing. There are some key elements that aren't even tied to budget because the same hundred sheets of paper can be the two million dollar script or the two hundred dollar script. It's the talent involved in the case of something like a screenplay. But, once you get on set, money buys you days, technology and there is something cool about that. It's certainly not an even playing field when it comes to comparing my little shows to big studio films, but they all do wind up on the video store shelves at some point.

I'm really proud of my most recent picture. It's a movie called *Dangerous Worry Dolls*, which was made for well under two hundred thousand dollars. You can look at any horror film put out by a major studio and figure they spent between twenty and fifty million dollars to get it made. I'm happy to do what I'm doing, this is my world and I've never looked over there and thought, "Oh, wouldn't it be nice to go with big studios." I don't necessarily have the tools or the money. There's a lot of things I don't have actually, but we have a ton of freedom and we really don't have to answer to anyone. We're still kind of victims of market conditions. To wake up and be independent to make certain kinds of film, to actually get those films made and get them out there within four or five months — that's the greatest part of being so independent and having our own little distribution channel.

You know, sometimes you may think to yourself, "Gosh, I'm shooting this movie in seven days. It would be great to have three more days." You realize that the big films sometimes shoot for half a year; 180 to a 200-day schedule. So, really it's apples and oranges, but I'm happy to have been independent for so long and I think the world is spinning towards the ability to make edgier content and get it out there through a delivery system that isn't fully stacked in the favor of the major studios.

Today, DVD distribution is next to impossible because your fifteen hundred thousand dollar movie that played theatrically is just not getting on the stores shelves and there aren't any tiny, little stores left anymore that will carry the independent products. The next frontier is digital distribution. I thought it was very significant that around two weeks ago for the first time in around ten or fifteen years, Wal-Mart lost their position as the biggest retailer of music to I-Tunes. I-Tunes is in its infancy. It's the tip of an iceberg that didn't even exist a few years ago and it has now generated more money, I don't know what the quarter was for the year with the exact time line, but they past Wal-Mart in terms of Wal-Mart selling hard goods. So, that bodes real well for people like me down the line. It may take a few more years, but the idea of putting up a library of my films on something similar to I-Tunes one day soon and if enough people are there for downloading or renting films, I see it as a very good thing.

**How about distributing films that are only available as direct Internet content?**

If there is still life left in DVD it still makes sense because you still have places like Blockbuster buying them and putting your titles on their shelves. It's not so much as the exclusion of DVD, but I see it as just being another delivery system. The world used to be really easy when I started off. You made some prints and you tried to get them onto the B-side of a double bill. Hopefully, we'd make a profit and the only other revenue, back in the day, was maybe a little television syndication. That was it; there was no other way to make a penny. This was before home video even.

Today, it is just so fragmented. You'd think that it would be very profitable, like the heyday, but most of these systems you just can't get into for all sorts of reasons. Hopefully, that's all going to change. I think the Internet and all the various forms of digital delivery will be just another great way to get your product out there. Theoretically, if it becomes as easy and as widely accepted as I-Tunes is becoming, then it's going to be easy for anyone to take advantage of that outlet. If somebody sees one of my movies and feels that film was enjoyable, they can go on a website like IMDB and discover I've done over 270 movies, but it's really, really hard to find some of those films. If it's easy to find all of them and the next step is something like I-Tunes, that, I think, makes the prospect simply amazing.

Again, the world has got to catch up with this concept. I'm in the business and I don't watch any movies on I-Tunes. I'll download music. I will do that. If I want to see a movie, I'll go find a DVD. So, I'm not even in that habit, but there are people who are watching them on their cell phones or computer screens. There is a real business being done that way. It may take several more years, but there will be a point where it's so easy to avoid driving down to your local video store. If it becomes unbelievably easy for anyone to pop into a universe of title lists, push a button and then ten minutes later they can either burn a DVD or it's on their hard drive… that makes sense to me.

**How about filming on digital video? Do you enjoy that outlook?**

I think it's okay. I'm a film guy and I only recently started filming my movies on Hi-Def. That decision was made only because I'm lucky enough to have a director of photography who does such a great job of making it look like it was shot on film. It's a bit of a sleight of hand trick. You know, up until about four movies ago, I shot everything on film. But, money was wasted and then you wind up with this entire film negative that never gets used or serves another purpose. It just sits somewhere and you have to spend money to store it. We are so in a digital world that it just doesn't make much sense anymore, in a way. I wouldn't have gone over to the other side if not for the fact that at the last two road shows, I had people still thinking I was shooting on film because the technology is pretty good, but also it's the talent involved. It's having a director of photography who really knows how to paint a picture and make it still look like you've shot the movie using film.

***Which of your films was the biggest financial success for you?***

The biggest financial hit for me was a movie called *Ghoulies*, and part of that success was because everything was kind of lined up just perfect at the time. That was released back when we were still taking movies out theatrically. It was a real hit. It didn't do a gazillion dollars for us, but it was singularly the most successful in terms of returns on investments. Now, the most successful series for me has been *The Puppet Master* series, by far. We haven't even scratched the surface with that series because we are now in discussions with people who want to fund a big, grown-up theatrical movie. Which, I haven't done in years and I felt like *Puppet Master* was the perfect franchise to make into a theatrical feature. I'm planning to do it in 3-D.

***What can you tell me about your latest project,*** **Dangerous Worry Dolls***?*

We are going to have like six releases coming up and that's the most current one. I have been a fan of the better, well-made women in prison movies and none of those have been made in awhile, so I decided to mix that genre with a visceral, edgy horror film. If you go to the site (**fullmoondirect.com**), there's a trailer up and you have to scroll down a bit to view it. I'm also very happy with the way the trailer turned out, as well.

It's kind of hard to describe that film, except that if you know what a worry doll is, a lot of people do and a lot of people don't. They come from Guatemala and they're pretty widely known throughout most of the country. They are these little half-inch tall dolls that usually come in this small, little wooden box. They're different characters, usually a man, woman, child and sometimes a dwarf. The legend goes that you put these dolls under your pillow at night and they make all your worries go away. So, I thought, what a cool idea to take that and turn that one around and create something kind of crazy. I think it's an example of a very small movie that was shot in seven days on a very modest budget. It just shows that you can do some quality work with great talent and very little money. I like that fact. I'm very excited about it and the road show. I'm sort of becoming like the Barnum and Bailey of horror, I guess.

# Greydon Clark
## by Mike White

**EDITOR'S NOTE**: Greydon Clark began his film career as an actor, appearing in Al Adamson's *Satan's Sadists*, *Hell's Bloody Devils*, and *Dracula vs. Frankenstein*. As a director he is best known for such films as *Black Shampoo*, *Satan's Cheerleaders*, and *The Forbidden Dance*.

*Thank you for taking the time to talk to me. I can't tell you how excited I am to have both you and John Daniels in this issue. Have you kept in touch with him? I'd love if a DVD of* Black Shampoo *came out with you two doing an audio commentary track.*

I've not been in contact with John Daniels for many years. I'd love to see or speak to him. It was a very good experience working with him and I have nothing but fond memories of him as a person and performer. I also would hope to do a commentary with him.

*Can you tell me about some of the cast of* Black Shampoo? *I've always wondered about some of the actors with some of the more outrageous screen names such as Jack Mehoff and Salvator Benissimo.*

The actor playing Jack Mehoff was a good friend who also was in those early pictures I've mentioned above. His name was Bill Bonner. Unfortunately, tragedy struck Bill very early in his life. In early 1976, not long after *Black Shampoo* while filming in the midwest, Bill was involved in an automobile accident and paralyzed. Jackie and I visited him for several months in the hospital. One day, he checked himself out without notice and literally disappeared. Bill was an exceptional actor and good friend. We tried to find him, but were unable to. Nobody ever saw him again.

Salvator Benissimo was Sheldon Lee. Sheldon worked in several of my earlier movies.

**Was that Jackie Cole from Satan's Cheerleaders and Angel's Brigade (also known as Angel's Revenge)?**

Jackie and I were together for more than 34 years. She was my wife and the mother of our two boys. She starred in *Satan's Sadists* under the name Jackie Taylor. I wrote and acted in *Satan's Sadists* for Al Adamson in 1968 and that's when Jackie and I first got together. She starred in the first movie I directed in 1970, *Mothers, Fathers and Lovers* and my second in 1973, *The Bad Bunch*.

*Black Shampoo* was my third movie and was made in 1975. It was not a SAG picture therefore many of the actors used alternate names. She used the name "Edith Wheeler." I've made 20 movies in my career and she was in many of them.

Jackie passed away in February of this year. She is loved and missed by all who knew her.

**How did you get your start in film?**

I came to Los Angeles in 1965, no experience, didn't know a soul. I wanted to be a "movie actor" and found the name of an acting coach in a book, *The Young Actors' Guide to Hollywood*. I attended classes for a couple of years. I sold various items door to door to put food on the table and pay for acting lessons. I met Al Adamson in 1967 through an actress I'd met in class. We became friends and he gave me my first role, a very small part in *The Fakers*.

Al owned the rights to a western short story he wanted written into a full length script. I volunteered to write it. I'd never written anything before, but after a few months, I presented the final script and it was very well received. Robert Taylor, a super star from MGM's heyday, agreed to star. ABC agreed to finance as one of their first movie-of-the-weeks. We were set to begin production in Spain in the spring of 1968 when Mr. Taylor suddenly entered the hospital with cancer. He died in a very short time and the project was never produced. A financier approached Al with $50,000 to produce a movie. We couldn't begin to do the western for that amount, but I convinced Al that I could write a script that could be done on that budget.

Motorcycle pictures were very popular at the time. This was just prior to *Easy Rider*. The picture was made in Indio, California, a desert community near Palm Springs. This was my first real picture making experience and I loved it. I had met Jackie in the same acting class and was instrumental in her being cast as the female star in *Satan's Sadists*.

The picture was an enormous success and played all over the world. I wrote a script about a Vietnam vet who returns to the states and rebels against the establishment. I decided I wanted to direct as well as act. Jackie and I starred in that picture, *Mothers, Fathers & Lovers*. We made that picture on a record low budget — $12,500! It had modest success. I'd like to think it was ahead of its time.

I was active in the civil rights movement of the late '60s and decided to write a story about a well meaning white guy who gets involved in the inner-city. *The Bad Bunch* also had a degree of success and we played in most major markets. The year was 1975 and I wanted to make another picture looking at the black experience, but did not want to make one where the hero was a pimp, pusher, cop, etc. I got the idea to make the hero a successful black businessman. *Shampoo* was about to come out with a ton of publicity.

*Black Shampoo* — a businessman who innocently gets involved with mobsters — it seemed like a good idea at the time. The picture played all over the world and was quite successful. From there, I was fortunate enough to make 17 more pictures, and still counting!

**So Mothers, Fathers & Lovers *is not the same as* The Bad Bunch? *I had read that they were the same movie.***

I consider *Mothers, Fathers & Lovers* to be a separate film from *The Bad Bunch*. They do share some of the same cast and a few scenes.

**You definitely were ahead of the times with your horror parody Wacko. *A lot of the elements in it seemed to echo through* Student Bodies, Scary Movie, *et cetera*.**

*Wacko* was my first picture with Joe Don Baker. When I was making the deal with him I could only afford him for two weeks. He asked how I could film him in two weeks. I explained that I would use a double for two weeks when he was in the "pumpkin head". He agreed to do the movie, but only if he was the only actor playing the Halloween Killer . . . .. And he'd do it for the two-week price.

Joe Don is a terrific actor and wonderful person. We did three films together and I have nothing but fond memories of our days together. Our last picture was *Final Justice*. Filmed entirely in Malta, it was a unique experience. Unfortunately, we've sort of lost contact over the years.

**You've worked with a lot of "name" actors; George Kennedy, Jack Palance, Martin Landau, Tony Curtis, et cetera. How is it managing "bigger" and "smaller" actors all on the same set?**

I've been very lucky regarding my relationships with actors. I've never really had difficulty, especially with "name" actors. I remember when I hired Jack Palance for the first time in *Angel's Brigade*. There were stories that he was difficult to work with. Nothing could be further from the truth. He was extremely well prepared, very cooperative and helpful with some of the young actors he was working with. Same is true with George Kennedy and Martin Landau. I remember on *Without Warning*, Marty worked almost 20 hours straight and never complained. George Kennedy agreed to come in for a quick shot on a day that he was not even paid for!

Wings Hauser came in after he was wrapped to do off-camera lines for Susan Blakely's close-up on *Sight Unseen*. These guys and many like them always put the picture before anything else. Their success is deserved, all real pros. I loved making all my pictures. Some were more successful than others, but all were a joy to make. I've been very fortunate in my career and have worked with many people who have gone on to wonderful careers.

*What are you working on currently?*

I've got a couple of projects, but nothing definite at this time. I don't like to talk about a project until it's an absolute "go."

In the last decade or so I've made four movies in Russia and one in Bulgaria. After doing *The Forbidden Dance* for Menachem Golan, this in itself was quite an experience. Ninety days from our first meeting (without even a story) to a Columbia Pictures national release. Menachem then asked me to go to Russia where I made *Dance Macabre* and *Mad Dog Coll* (aka *Killer Instinct*) for him. I made *Russian Holiday* and *Dark Future* for my own company in St. Petersburg. *Star Games* was made in Bulgaria for my own company. It is very interesting shooting overseas, especially in former communist nations. I also made two episodes of *The New Mike Hammer*.

*Do you have anything you can share with other die hard* **Black Shampoo** *fans?*

A day before shooting began my cameraman was in an automobile accident. Nothing too serious, but he received a blow to his face. He insisted he was okay, but within the first few hours of shooting he came to me and said he couldn't continue. He suggested that the gaffer could shoot the film. The gaffer was Dean Cundey. He'd never shot a movie before. Necessity, being that mother, I gave him a chance. Dean ended up shooting *Satan's Cheerleaders, The Hi-Riders, Angel's Brigade* and *Without Warning* for me. As you know Dean is one of the most successful directors of photography in the last two decades with credits on major films too numerous to mention.

*Of all your work, what film are you the most proud of?*

I'm proud of all my work and it would be impossible to pick a favorite. If pushed, I'd say, "The next one."

# Larry Cohen
## by Andrew J. Rausch

With a career spanning five decades, screenwriter, producer, and director Larry Cohen has established himself as one of the most versatile and prolific individuals ever to work in the medium. He has written and directed pictures in nearly every genre conceivable, and his rather impressive filmography bears this out.

In 1970, Cohen made his directorial debut with the film *Bone*. Because he pulled a terrific performance out of leading man Yaphet Kotto, the studios saw him as a white director who could work well with black actors. Based on this, Cohen soon crafted a gangster film for Sammy Davis Jr. When the project fell apart, Cohen shot the film as a blaxploitation picture for American International Pictures. The resulting film, *Black Caesar* — a retooling of classic Warner Bros. gangster films such as *Little Caesar* — would ultimately be one of the finest films to emerge from the genre. The film would also solidify lead actor Fred Williamson's standing as one of the genre's greatest stars.

Despite the fact that *Black Caesar's* protagonist, Tommy Gibbs, dies at the end of the film, the studio soon sent Cohen and Williamson back out to shoot a sequel, *Hell Up in Harlem*. This film would not be quite as solid as its predecessor, but it made a killing at the box office and would ultimately become one of the genre's most popular titles.

Cohen's other screenwriting credits include *The Return of the Magnificent Seven*, *El Condor*, *Phone Booth*, and *Cellular*. His directorial credits include *It's Alive!*, *God Told Me To*, *Best Seller*, and the blaxploitation reunion film *Original Gangstas*. In addition, Cohen has written extensively for television and has even created the cult television series *Branded* and *The Invaders*.

**There has always been quite a bit of debate over the term blaxploitation. Some people find it offensive, while others, such as Quentin Tarantino, look at it more in terms of other exploitation films, such as women-in-prison films and the early bootlegging films of Burt Reynolds. What does the term blaxploitation mean to you?**

*Every* movie is an exploitation movie. Every movie tries to get you to part with your eight dollars. Our job is to get you to spend your money, and come into the theater, not unlike a barker at a carnival sideshow trying to entice you to come and see the fat lady or the dwarf. That's what the whole business is about. You do whatever you have to do to sell tickets. Every picture is exploiting something and some audience. So what if you're making films for a black audience? Why shouldn't they have their cinema, anyway? There was a long period when there were no black pictures. So, as soon as they started making pictures for a black audience, somebody went around yelling, "Blaxploitation!" It's rather foolish, obviously. I think it tainted the product, and people didn't look at the pictures more clearly until later on. I guess Quentin Tarantino had something to do with the reemergence of black film, because he said a few nice things about the pictures and people started seeing them again.

*Black Caesar* is really not any different from those Warner Bros. films, like *Little Caesar* and *The Public Enemy*. It really is the same kind of a story about the rise and fall of an American gangster. It's not really your typical black exploitation film, where the black hero wins every fight, wins the woman, and gets everything. In *Black Caesar*, he loses everything and ends up in the gutter. He loses the woman who betrayed him, and he loses his entire empire. So, in that respect, it's really more like *Public Enemy* or *Little Caesar*.

**How did Black Caesar come about?**

Sammy Davis Jr. was looking for a picture in which he could play the lead, rather than playing a stooge for Dean Martin and Frank Sinatra. He felt he was ready for a starring role of his own. So his manager, Sy Marsh, contacted me. He said they'd pay $10,000 for a treatment for a movie that Sammy could play in. I said, "How about doing a gangster movie?" Sammy was a little guy, but so was Edward G. Robinson and James Cagney. They were great as gangsters, and I felt we could do a black gangster movie. The rise and fall of a Harlem gangster. Of course it took another 35 years for them to make *American Gangster* with Denzel Washington.

So anyway, I wrote the treatment, and when it came time to collect my $10,000, Sammy was not paying. His manager said he was having trouble with the Internal Revenue Service, he didn't have any money, and he couldn't pay. So I was stuck with the treatment *Black Caesar*.

And then I went in to see Sam Arkoff at American International, and they'd seen a previous movie I'd done called *Bone*. He was impressed with the movie, and with the performance of Yaphet Kotto, so he said, "We're looking for some black product like *Shaft* and *Superfly*. Have you got anything?" I said, "You came to the right person." I ran downstairs and got it out of the trunk of my car and brought it up. And we had a deal right there. So we were already off and rolling immediately — all thanks to Sammy Davis Jr.

**Was the original treatment you wrote for Sammy Davis Jr. much different from the film you ultimately shot?**

No. It was pretty much the same. Of course Fred Williamson brought something different to it; he brought glamour to it. Fred was a good-looking guy. You know, he wore the clothes beautifully. He was great. He looked very much like Denzel looked in the modern version of the picture. There are a lot of similarities there. The shots look almost identical in the ad campaign shots, with him dressed up in his snazzy suit.

**Did the critics or the studios tend to treat the blaxploitation films differently than they treated other pictures?**

Well, you know, the critics never tended to treat any of the American International pictures favorable. These were all "B" movies, and they fulfilled a function of appealing to a certain specific kind of audience. I think sometimes they might have been better than the "A" pictures. But they were never expected to get any critical raves. They were just expected to make some money, to generate some activity at the box office. So I wasn't disappointed. To tell you the truth, the reviews for *Black Caesar* were actually pretty good. They were better than they were for most AIP movies, but this was a better movie. It was a better script. It was a "B" movie, but it had an "A" quality script.

***I've always felt that* Black Caesar *holds up a lot better than some of the other blaxploitation pictures.***

A lot of the other pictures are just a lot of brutality — a lot of going out and shooting people. You know, Pam Grier's gonna go out and blow people away and stab them in the groin. It was just monotonous and vulgar. Our picture had its share of violence, but it all had something to do with the integral storyline or integral racism of America. You know, the picture was about crooked New York cops, and, as it turns out, there really were crooked New York cops. It was about using teenage kids to run drugs and money in the underworld manipulated by the police department. And it turns out it was true. They were using teenage black kids to do that. All the stuff I made up turned out to be true. I just basically concocted what turned out to be the truth.

***Most blaxploitation films written by white screenwriters tended to have a lot of "jive talk," which didn't ring true. It sounded forced. I notice there isn't much of that in* Black Caesar.**

As I said, this was a good quality script. Also, in working with the actors, I kind of let them get comfortable with the lines. If they wanted to change something or put it into their own words, we did that. I wanted it to feel natural rather than forced, as you say. And the actors felt comfortable with it, too. They had a good time. I had a good time.

We shot up in Harlem. This was a period when some of the Hollywood movie companies were going up there to film movies like *Across 110th Street*, and they were shaken down by all the local black gangsters. "You can't shoot on this street unless you pay us." So when I got up there with my small crew, we were approached by these same hoods again. And I didn't have any money to pay them, so I said to them, "You guys are great. You ever think of doing any acting? You'd be great as Fred Williamson's guys." So we recruited all these fellas who were members of a gang and put them in the picture. I even had them put into the ad campaign, on the poster. After that, we owned Harlem. We never had any problem doing anything we wanted. Opening day at the Cinerama Theater, there were all these black gangsters standing around the theater, signing autographs. It was a very enjoyable shoot.

*Did you sit in on any of the screenings?*
The first screening we had at the Pantages Theater was a disaster. Everybody loved the picture, but they hated the ending where Fred died. In the original version, he was killed by a gang of street kids who stole his wristwatch and everything. They didn't know he was the godfather of Harlem; they just thought he was some dressed-up guy staggering injured through the streets of Harlem. They descend upon him like a pack of wolves and they kill him. When that happened, a lot of people in the audience — the black audience in particular — got angry. One black woman was screaming at me in the lobby. "Black people wouldn't do this to their own kind!" That is, of course, an erroneous comment, since most killings of black people in the black community are committed by black gangs and other members of the black community. Black people are the most common victims of black crime. What she said certainly wasn't true, but I called up Arkoff and I said, "Sam, we're in terrible trouble. We're opening this picture in a couple of days and the audience just hates the ending." He says, "Well, I told you not to kill him at the end." So I said, "Sam, we've got to do something about this." He said, "Well, what do you want to do?" I said, "I've got to take out the ending. We'll just have to cut the ending off."

So, with his permission, I went to New York where we were going to open first. I went to the Cinerama Theater the morning the picture was gonna open. I went to the projectionist and identified myself. We went upstairs and we cut off the last scene of the picture. Then I went across town to another theater on 59th Street and introduced myself to the manager there. We then went up and cut off the last minute of the picture. We then went up to 86th Street and did the same thing. And the picture opened to be a huge success. Really big. I mean, they started putting in 3 a.m. shows. The theater was closed for maybe three hours a day. They were running the picture continuously all day long. They raised the ticket prices by a dollar after the first couple of days. There was a line around the block. It was February, freezing cold, and the lines were up around the block. The police had those wooden horses put up, and people were waiting for an hour, hour and a half to see the picture. I thought, Wow, this is great. Every movie is gonna be like this! Of course I was wrong, but... Cutting off the ending really just took a disaster and turned it into a success.

Then videos and DVDs were made years later, and they went back to the original negative, which hadn't been cut. So now he dies at the end. The DVD and the VHS have the original ending. And in the foreign version, which were again made from the original negative rather than the cut negative, he also dies at the end. So there are two versions of the movie — the home video version and the theatrical cut.

*I'm going to name some of the people you worked with on* Black Caesar *and* Hell Up in Harlem, *and I'd like you to comment on each of them.*

Okay.

*Fred Williamson.*

I worked with Fred three times. The third film on which I worked with him was *Original Gangstas*, which he produced. And it was entirely different working with him as a producer than it was working with him as an actor. As a producer, he was now saddled with the financial responsibilities. And that made him extremely nervous and tense and concerned. So I didn't have the same devil-may-care relationship with him that I did on the first two pictures, where it was mainly just having fun. I'd say, "Look at that great big sign over Times Square. Let's climb up to the top of it and shoot a scene up there." He'd say, "Okay, Cohen, you do it first." And I'd have to climb up to the top of the sign and do it. And then naturally he wouldn't want to lose face in front of the crew, so if I would do it, he would do it. I said, "Okay, Fred, when the cab rounds the corner, I want you to jump out and roll on the sidewalk." And he said, "Yeah, sure, I'm gonna throw myself out on the sidewalk out of a taxi cab! You do it." So I would throw myself out of a taxi cab, jump up from the ground with a big smile on my face, and say, "Nothing to it." Then I'd go around the corner and scream in agony. So then he would do the same damn thing! He'd jump out of the cab, and he'd jump up and brush himself off, a big grin on his face. Then he'd go up the street and go into a doorway and scream in agony. Neither of us wanted to show the other one that we were in any way chicken. So we did all kinds of stuff like that. In one scene, I had myself picked up by some apparatus and then buried in a pile of coal. And he said, "I'm gonna get my legs chopped off if I try to do that!" I said, "No, you're too tall anyway, Fred! If I can do it, you can do it." We had a lot of fun doing those two pictures.

But later on, when he hired me to do the directing on *Original Gangstas*, it was a bit different because he was worried about getting his money. And his money was predicated on bringing the picture in under budget. And my interest was making the best picture possible. So we were a little bit at odds. Fred was really responsible for a lot of the success of that picture. He cast all the actors — not only the stars, but also the supporting players. He dug them all up, and they were all very good. And he found all the locations in Gary, Indiana, and arranged everything down there. Basically all I had to do was go in and direct the picture and make some sense out of the story. Sometimes it didn't make much sense in the script that he had, so I had to go in and rewrite it. It was a tough shoot because it was probably 106 degrees every day, and we had no air conditioning. Fred wouldn't spring for air conditioning. We had our problems there, but we made what I thought was a very good picture. And it actually got good reviews when it came out. Of the three pictures, I think that was the best reviewed. I hope it's because I've gotten better as a director over the 20 years between them.

*Gloria Hendry.*

Well, Gloria worked on the two *Black Caesar* pictures. She was a very nice person. A very pretty, very athletic young girl. Never any problems. Always eager to please. She's still a friend to this day. I see her sometimes at these retrospectives, and she's so happy to see me, and she has nothing but very pleasant memories of the pictures. And again, she was the type of person who would do anything you needed them to do. You know, run through the streets of New York, run through the theater district. I'd say, "Run into that empty theater, Gloria, and run down the aisle. We're gonna run into the theater after you." And this was without any permission or anything. And we did it. We shot scenes in all kinds of places we weren't supposed to be, but nobody stopped us. So she was game for anything. What can you say when you have somebody who'll try anything you ask them to do? You've got to like them, and I did like her. She was a swell girl.

*D'Urville Martin.*

D'Urville Martin was a friend of Fred Williamson's. He'd been in a couple of Fred Williamson pictures before ours. He was kind of a swinging kind of guy. You know, I never knew what was going on with people. I don't know if they were smoking grass or taking dope or what. I never even thought about it. I just made my movie. So I don't know what the hell D'Urville was up to. But he always seemed to be happy. One day I did have some trouble with him. He got hostile one day. I don't know why. So I told him to lie down on the ground, I wanted to get a shot of him on the ground. He didn't know what the hell it was for. So he lay down on the ground and I shot a shot of him. Then after I got it, I told him, "Now you're dead. So if you give me any more trouble on this picture, I've already filmed your death." And I never had any trouble from him again. Not a peep.

**Julius Harris.**

Julius was in a lot of my pictures. I think Julius was a very, very gifted actor. He was wonderful as the father in *Black Caesar*. He brought a whole different dimension to the role. It was because of him that I wrote the part of the father into the sequel *Hell Up in Harlem*, where I really elaborated on the father's character. There he evolved from a common everyman to Big Poppa, the heir apparent to the underworld regime that Fred Williamson advocated. So I built up a big part for him in the second picture.

We had a lot of fun together. One time we took him to the Copa to see Sara Vaughan in New York. We liked him. Anytime we ran into Julius, he was always very, very happy to see me. I must say that about most of the actors. I've very seldom had any actor who didn't seem delighted when I ran into them and want to reminisce about the experience.

**Gloria Hendry told me you actually shot some of Black Caesar in your own home. Is that right?**

Oh, yeah. The big mansion in California was actually shot at my house. Then we shot a scene in *Hell Up in Harlem* where it was supposed to be a church — that was my house. For a scene that was supposed to be a nightclub, I turned my living room into a nightclub by putting up curtains and putting up tables. The scene where the district attorney gets hanged was shot out in my yard amongst the big trees. He's supposed to be outside of a church, but really that was in front of my house. In *Black Caesar*, the scene with Fred Williamson's office and with the lawyer's office were all shot in my basement. The scene with D'Urville Martin's dressing room in the church was actually shot in my basement.

I have a big house, and we had a lot of flats we could put up and make sets out of. So I preferred to shoot at home rather than to go rent studio space. I didn't have to go to work in the morning; I could just stay home. And they shot up the house pretty good in *Hell Up in Harlem*, too. There was an attack on the house. They were firing machine guns off and all kinds of shit. At least we didn't do any damage.

I was making these pictures for a set price. And if I brought the picture in cheaper, I got to keep the money, so why not put money into your pocket rather than give it to some studio?

**You worked with James Brown on the soundtrack to Black Caesar. What was that experience like?**

That was kind of a comical experience. James was wonderful, but he'd never written the music for a movie before. So we gave him a print of the picture and gave him the timings of the scenes. He went off and made the music and recorded it, sang it with his backup singers and everything. His manager, Charles Bobbitt, came to me with all the tapes. We transferred them all to film and played them with all the scenes. Unfortunately, if the scene was five minutes long, James wrote seven minutes' worth of music. If the scene was six minutes long, James wrote nine minutes' worth of music. If it was a one-minute scene, he wrote two or three minutes. So I called up Bobbitt and I said, "This is what he did: if the scene was two minutes, he gave me five minutes' worth of music." Bobbitt says, "Well, then you have more than you need." I said, "It doesn't work that way, Charles. The music is supposed to fit the scene." So finally I had to go and get a music editor, and I sat there myself and cut and edited all the music cues down so they fit the sequences. I never told American International what happened. I just fixed it myself and gave them the finished picture. They were very happy. They were so happy, in fact, that they hired James to make music for *Slaughter's Big Rip-Off* with James Brown. And he did the same thing to them again! But this time they found out about it, and they didn't have me to fix it. So they went out of their minds about it. They were gonna sue him. It was a terrible mess.

So when time came to do *Hell Up in Harlem*, I wanted to use James Brown again. And they said, "Absolutely under no circumstances will we ever work with James Brown again." I said, "He did the music for *Black Caesar*, it's great music." But they said, "No, we will not hire James Brown again! The only way we could do it is if James Brown wrote the whole thing on spec. If we like it, we'll use it." So I went back to Bobbitt and said, "That's the only way they'll do it." So the next day, I get a call from Bobbitt and he says, "The man accepts the challenge. He will write the entire score for the picture, record it and give it to you, and if you like it you can use it. If you don't like it, you don't have to use it." That was the most amazing offer I'd ever heard from a big-name artist like James Brown. He did just that. He wrote the music for the film, which was going to be titled *Black Caesar's Revenge*. And American International heard it and they said, "Ah, it's the same old James Brown stuff again. We've got a deal cooking with Motown, and we don't want the James Brown music." I tried to convince them but they wouldn't listen. So I called up Bobbit. He said, "It's okay. We'll just take the music back and we'll use it somewhere else." And sure enough he did. James Brown put out an album called *Payback*, which became his most successful album. And not only was it a big successful album, but years later it was used as the musical score for a film called *Lock, Stock, and Two Smoking Barrels* (1998). So all the music that was written for me, with all the lyrics that applied to *Black Caesar's* sequel, all ended up in their film. We lost out on getting the most successful album James ever had, and we ended up with a second-rate Motown score. It wasn't bad, but we'd have been much better off with the James Brown score.

But what can you do? You know, you can't fight city hall. And that was the only time I had any interference from American International on either picture. They were just adamant about not giving any more business to James Brown.

*I've heard there were a lot of scheduling conflicts when you shot* **Hell Up in Harlem***, so you had to shoot primarily on the weekends. Is that right?*

Well, Fred was not available because he was doing *That Man Bolt* for Universal. He was going to be on that picture for a number of months, and Arkoff wanted to get a sequel and get it out there so he could capitalize. So I said, "The only way we can do it is to shoot it on the weekends. I'm shooting a picture for Warner Bros. called *It's Alive!*, and I'm shooting five days a week. I could shoot Saturday and Sunday on *Hell Up in Harlem*. So that's what we did. We ended up shooting seven days a week. I used mostly the same crew as well as the sound editor on *It's Alive!* and *Hell Up in Harlem*. It was a madhouse. The poor editor didn't know from one day to the next what picture he was cutting. He wasn't sure what he was doing, but I was standing there next to him, so he got through it. We shot the picture mainly on the weekends, and then when we went to New York without Fred, we used a double. Then we shot all the reverse shots of Fred out in California. You have to know exactly what you're doing when you make a picture like that. You have to know exactly what every shot is going to look like, and what every cut is gonna look like. I carried the whole picture in my head so I could do it. I don't think I would recommend this to other people. But I did it, and I made it work.

*I was amazed when I learned that you used a body double to such great lengths. You can't tell at all.*

Fred didn't like the double. He thought the double's ass was too fat. He was pissed off. He said, "Where'd you get the fat ass on that guy?" I said, "Look, Fred, no one knows it's not you. Just cool it. Nobody will ever know."

We actually got Fred back to New York a few days here and there, even though he was still under contract to Universal. One day we were shooting in the American Airlines terminal in New York City, and right in the middle of shooting Lew Wasserman — the president of MCA/Universal — walks up to me! "Hi, boys," said Lew Wasserman. "What are you shooting?" I'm thinking to myself, I wonder if he's gonna realize that this actor is under contract to him. We were in conflict here. So I just said to Mr. Wasserman, "You wanna be in the picture?" I tried to talk him into being one of the gangsters. He was so busy getting out of that one that he never really found out what picture we were making.

# Roger Corman
## by Andrew J. Rausch

Roger Corman is easily one of the most prolific auteurs in the history of the film industry. Corman has produced or directed nearly 300 films to date. He began directing in 1955, sometimes churning out as many as eight films a year. He is best remembered for the cult classic *The Little Shop of Horrors*, which he shot in only two days, as well as a string of impressive Edgar Allan Poe adaptations that starred the late Vincent Price.

In 1971 Corman retired from directing (although he would return to direct Frankenstein Unbound in 1990) to focus on producing and distributing films. Corman has produced over 250 films including *Dementia 13*, *The Big Doll House*, *Ride In the Whirlwind*, and *Humanoids from the Deep*. Corman has appeared as an actor in over 20 films including *Apollo 13*, *Philadelphia*, *The Silence of the Lambs*, and *The Godfather, Part II*. Besides being the undisputed king of the exploitation market, Corman will be remembered for having an eye for talent, discovering *many* talented young filmmakers, including Martin Scorsese, Francis Ford Coppola, and James Cameron.

It's 10:10 as film critic Michael Dequina and I arrive at Roger Corman's Brentwood office. After making a mad dash across the city, we're 10 minutes late. Anywhere else in the world this would be considered a bad thing, but in Los Angeles, being late is considered fashionable. Walking through the plush office building, we are surrounded by scores of posters for oddball B-movies such as the aforementioned *Humanoids from the Deep*, assuring us that we're in the right place. An assistant asks us to have a seat. Soon Mr. Corman makes his entrance and leads us to his office, which has sort of a minimalist look.

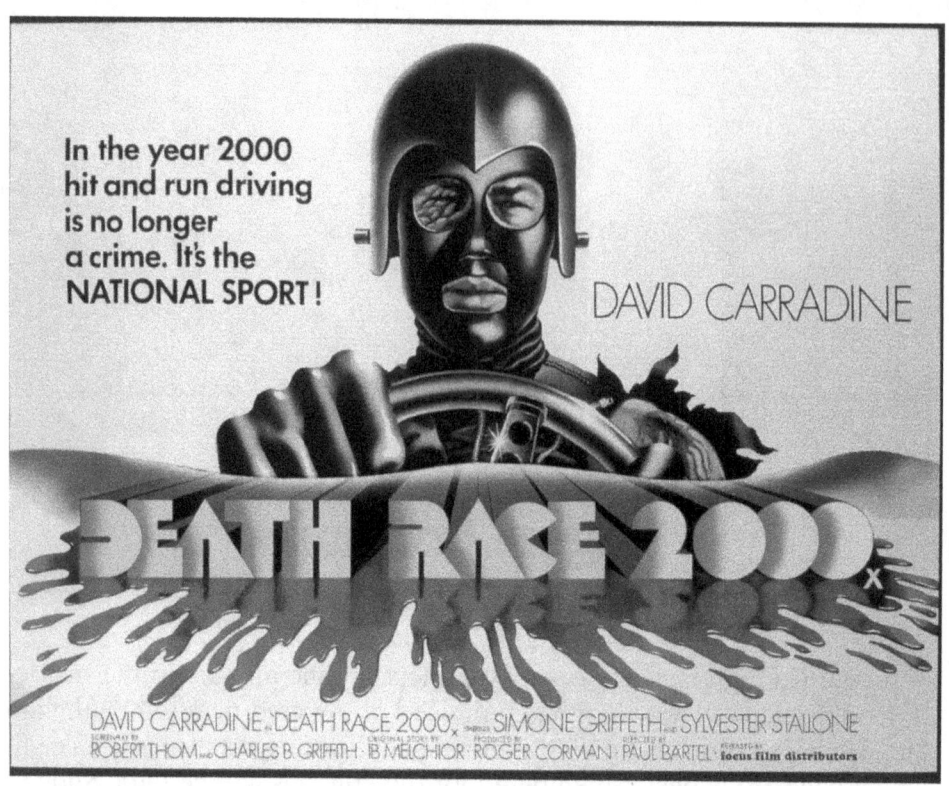

Corman is a well-dressed man who shows no signs of aging. I find him to be sharp as a tack, throwing out names and dates with the greatest of ease. (Of course these are *his* films, but there are nearly 300 of them!) With each question, he pauses a moment and carefully formulates his thoughts. Despite the fact he's probably been asked these same questions countless times before by other journalists, Corman obviously enjoys talking about his work. With the mention of each film or star he's been involved with, his smile grows wider.

*As a filmmaker/producer who has made a career out of making primarily low-budget independent films, what are your thoughts on the recent film* **The Blair Witch Project?**

I think *The Blair Witch Project* is an exceptionally well-conceived and well-made film. It's well-conceived for this reason: they understood what their budget was and they wrote the script and made their picture to do the best possible job they could on that budget. One of the worst things you can do is have a limited budget and try to do some big looking film. That's when you end up with very bad work. They accepted their limitations and tailored their film to those limitations, which was the conception. Then with the execution, they did very well.

*Does the film signal the arrival of a new trend in the film industry?*

Yes. It will not affect the major pictures in any way, but it will and, in fact, is already affecting the very lowest budget films.

*You've been a part of the film industry for nearly five decades. What are some of the most significant changes you've seen over that time?*

Probably the biggest change I've seen has been the ever-growing dominance over theatrical exhibition by the major studios. When I started in the late 1950s, every film I made — no matter how low the budget — got a theatrical release. Today, less than 20 percent of our films get a theatrical release. The major studios have dominated the theatrical market. It started about 10 or 15 years ago and has rapidly increased over the past five years to the point where we are dependent primarily on home video, pay TV, and syndicated TV for our income.

*I'm going to read a quote by Quentin Tarantino to you and I'd like you to comment on it: "Roger Corman would find a young Jonathan Demme or Jonathan Kaplan or Joe Dante or Francis Coppola or Martin Scorsese and because they were hungry to make a movie, they'd make the best women-in-prison film ever."*

[Laughs.] In regards to that particular quote, Jonathan Demme is the only one who actually made a women-in-prison picture. But the statement is correct. We did a number of women-in-prison features in the 1970s. We did four or five of them, I think. Jonathan took that assignment [*Caged Heat*, 1971] and said exactly that: "This is gonna be the best one ever made." I think it indicated his enthusiasm and determination to make a good picture. The others did well, but they just took it as an assignment and said, "We'll just make this a prison feature," and just did it. Jonathan took the genre, worked with it, and made something exceptionally good. That indicated from the beginning that he had an extraordinary talent. I think the distinguishing characteristic of all of them, no matter what films they did — Francis Coppola did a horror film, Joe Dante did a satire of a horror film called *Hollywood Boulevard* and then went on to do a science fiction horror film called *Pirahna* — is that they were all determined to do the best possible work they could do.

AR: *I'd like to name some of the filmmakers you've discovered and get you to comment on each of them.*

All right.

*Francis Ford Coppola.*

Francis Coppola came to me as a film editor out of UCLA film school and then advanced rapidly to eventually writing and directing his first film for me [*Dementia 13*, 1963]. He is one of the most brilliant all-around filmmakers I have ever met. When I say all-around, I mean that not only can he write and direct, but he can also edit, function as cameraman, and do almost every job connected with filmmaking.

**Jonathan Kaplan.**

Jonathan Kaplan came to me to do a very low-budget film about student nurses on the recommendation of Martin Scorsese, who had been a teacher of his at the NYU film school. Jonathan is a very good director who is particularly good at blending comedy with drama and action.

**Monte Hellman.**

Monte Hellman started as a stage director and editor before becoming a film director. He's one of the best directors I know at working with actors.

**Jack Hill.**

Jack Hill again is one of the better all-around filmmakers. He excels in three or four categories. He's a good writer, director, producer, editor, and cameraman.

**Peter Bogdanovich.**

Peter Bogdanovich has demonstrated brilliance both as a writer and as a director. His first film for me was *Targets*, which was one of the best debut films of any of the directors I've worked with.

**Jonathan Demme.**

Jonathan Demme has grown continually as a director. His first work was good and with each additional film he's gotten better, so he's gone from being merely a good director to a great director.

**James Cameron.**

Jim Cameron is proof that if you are good, you'll get promoted. He started with me as a model-maker on *Battle Beyond the Stars*. We were having trouble with the special effects and I sent my ace assistant Gale Ann Hurd down to the set to find out what was going wrong. She came back after a couple of days and said the staff is not as competent as they should be, but there's a young model-maker at the bottom of the list who knows more than anyone else. I went down to the set that day and promoted Jim Cameron and he was head of special effects and second director on the next picture, showing that if you have the ability, it will be recognized quickly.

**Joe Dante.**

Joe Dante started as a trailer editor and then moved up the traditional way from trailer editor to feature film editor to second unit director and then to director. I think he's one of the best directors in the country. While I have great admiration for Joe and everything he's done, I regret a little bit the fact that I've never, ever been able to find a trailer editor as good since he left! [Laughs.]

**Richard Matheson wrote the script for The Pit and the Pendulum. What was he like to work with?**

Richard Matheson is one of the best science fiction writers with his short stories, novels, and screenplays in the world, I believe. The beauty of working with Dick was that his first draft was almost a final draft. I spent so much time working with writers who would go through a first draft, a second draft, a third draft and you're still not there. You could have just one discussion with Dick about what the film was going to be about and he would then, by himself, come up with a first draft that was almost ready to shoot. With the possible exception of John Sayles, I don't think I've ever seen that in another writer.

**Martin Scorsese.**

Martin Scorsese is one of the few directors I gave an opportunity to direct without having worked for me as an assistant. I saw an underground film he'd made in New York, which I liked very much, and gave him the opportunity to do *Boxcar Bertha*. Once more, he tackled a subject he had no personal knowledge of, but he had the great intelligence and creativity to make it a great film.

**In Scorsese on Scorsese, Martin Scorsese remembers of Boxcar Bertha, "Roger just told me to read the script: 'Rewrite as much as you want, but remember Marty, you must have some nudity every 15 pages.'" Would you like to comment on that?**

[Laughs.] That's close, I think. The statement is almost correct. Needless to say we talked a little bit more than that and I didn't say every 15 pages. I think I said two or three times in the picture. [Laughs again.] He, possibly on his own, decided to do it every 15 pages, but I don't particularly remember saying that. He may be remembering the film being a little racier than it was. I think there was only nudity in there two or three times.

***Something else I remember reading was that you had expressed interest in financing*** Mean Streets *as a black exploitation film. Is that right?*

Yes. He came to me with the idea and I liked it, but at that time the black films were really very successful. I'd been thinking that I wanted to make a black film and I thought, this film would really work well as a black film. He then took most of my crew and what most people don't know about *Mean Streets* — even the New York critics commented on how much of a New York picture it was — he shot most of that picture in Los Angeles, utilizing my crew. It was a great Italian film, but it would have been just as great a black film!

*You directed Jack Nicholson in* The Little Shop of Horrors *and then produced a few films that he starred in. What was he like to work with?*

Jack was great to work with. He was a very focused, very dedicated, very intense actor who could bring a humanity and a humor to the most dramatic situations.

*And you shot* The Little Shop of Horrors *in just two days?*

[Grins broadly.] Two days and a night.

*That is almost unheard of. Especially by today's standards.*

I did it almost as a joke simply to see if I could do it. When I finished, Bob Towne, who is a good friend of mine, said, "You should remember, Roger, making films is not like a track meet. It's not how fast you go." [Laughs.] And I said, "You're right, Bob. I'll never make a two-day picture again."

*What did you think of the musical remake of* The Little Shop of Horrors?

I thought technically it was a good, big, well-made film. I liked it very much, but I thought maybe because of its budget, it lacked a little bit of the spontaneity and the humor that was in the original.

*You had a cameo in* The Godfather, Part II, *which is one of my favorite films. How did you become involved with that?*

Francis cast all members of the Senate investigations committee with writers, producers, and directors. He took us all to lunch on the first day we worked and I remember Bill Bowers, a comedy writer, asked him how he chose us. Francis said he had watched a Senate crime investigation committee on television and he said he noticed that all the Senators looked good and spoke intelligently. We all thought, Wow! That's pretty good! [Laughs.] And then he said, "And they all looked a little bit awkward on camera. So I thought people who were writers, directors, and producers would know what was going on and be able to look good and talk intelligently but because they weren't actors, they'd be a little awkward." Everybody was a little deflated but I thought, That's brilliant casting! That's exactly what we were.

# David F. Friedman
## by Nathaniel Thompson

**EDITOR'S NOTE:** Producer David F. Friedman met Herschell Gordon Lewis when Lewis was putting together financing for his first picture, *The Prime Time*. The two hit it off and Friedman then produced 11 films for Lewis, including *Blood Feast*, *Two Thousand Maniacs*, and *Color Me Blood Red*. Friedman then left Lewis to produce another 40 or so films, including the exploitation classics *Love Camp 7*, *The Erotic Adventures of Zorro*, and *Ilsa: She Wolf of the SS*. Friedman later collaborated with Lewis again on the 2002 film *Blood Feast 2: All U Can Eat*. Friedman died in 2011 at the age of 87.

*You came from a strong carnival/sideshow background that influenced your filmmaking. How much do you feel the two have in common?*
The whole milieu of exploitation, the old roadshow men like Dwain Esper and Lewis Sonney, had a background in the carny, or at times they'd be doing films and working carny at the same time. Go out somewhere with the carny and then in the winter go out with pictures; it went hand in glove. The whole idea of the roadshow was that you not only showed them a picture but sold them something else, like a book or a postcard, or you had a lobby display.

When I was a kid, this guy came through town with a "crime does not pay" show, and he had all of these guns in the lobby. A friend of mine named Mike Ripps made a picture years ago called *Bayou*, and he turned it over to United Artists. Mike was from Alabama like me. For a few years they didn't do anything with it since there wasn't anything to the picture, really. It was supposed to be about people living down in Louisiana. Mike took the picture back and came up with a great title — *Poor White Trash*.

Then he went out on the road, doing roadshows for this thing. He made a trailer himself in the background saying, "I was the producer of this picture. Due to the abnormal subject matter, only viewers over the age of 18 will be admitted. Armed guards will be at the box office to make certain that everyone is 18, and you must sign an affidavit stating you are over 18." So he's out roadshowing this thing with a couple of guys dressed like cops, and they got a printed affidavit for everybody to sign. You could play the actual picture at a Sunday school picnic, really. Mike made a great remark, though; "If you want to make a picture, they can see that on TV. You gotta give 'em a show. With me, they had the show before they ever even got into the theater."

That was basically what exploitation was all about — a happy combination of the carny and film business. With roadshows you could be in a few dozen places at the same time, and you didn't mind if it rained or not. If it rained on a carny, you were dead for the night. With a theater, though, it doesn't bother you too much. Loving both film and carny, it was a natural for me.

**It's interesting that you mention Dwain Esper and those guys. A lot of them had legal problems, mostly their own fault, with their cutthroat distribution.**

Oh, yeah, stealing prints and jumping their territory. In my book I talked about when Dwain bought the rights to *Freaks* from Mrs. Browning and had it out as *Forbidden Love*. The only forbidden love is between the midget and the full-grown woman! People were coming into a drive-in down in Charlotte, looking at a classic film, and they didn't know what they were looking at. They started tearing the damn theater apart, and Dwain runs into the projection booth with a reel of nudist camp stuff and says, "Quick, lace this up!" So the audience said, "Oh, wow, look at that!" All of a sudden you've got nudists running around for 15 minutes and everybody walks out of the joint well satisfied.

Those were the things that fascinated me, though I actually had a job with Paramount, climbing the corporate ladder, until I decided to get a little more excitement. That's when I hooked up with Kroger Babb and the boys at Modern Film in Chicago. As a matter of fact, I walked away from a pretty fair job; they'd offered to let me come to New York and head the publicity department of the company when I decided to go out roadshowing with *Mom and Dad* [and] *Because of Eve*. That took guts!

The old roadshow guys had a spirit of adventure, the guts of a burglar. These pictures could take any subject that the major companies couldn't touch at the time because of the Hays Code. As long as the subject was in bad taste, you could go out and exploit it. You had dope pictures, pictures about childbirth, miscegenation. Anything went.

Herschell Gordon Lewis and I had been making nudie cuties and nudist camp pictures, and we invented another genre that came to be known as the "roughie" with a planet called *Scum of the Earth*. It was deliberately shot in black-and-white as contrast to the la-di-da nudie cuties, to make it look like a little stag film. It brought in a little violence, too. Violence even more than sex became the principal ingredient of the roughie. You get a little tired of the beautiful young starlets in various stages of dress and undress, prancing around in nudie cuties, and nudist camp is about as erotic as going through the cold storage room at Swift & Co. So we were tossing around ideas one day and out of it came that four-letter word: gore.

That's where *Blood Feast* came about. Herschell and I were on our way down to Miami to make a nudist camp picture called *Bell, Bare and Beautiful*, with a stripper named Virginia Bell. On the way down, we started putting a script down on paper, and out of it came *Blood Feast*. When we had finished *Bell* for a bunch of burlesque people, we kept half a dozen of those folks to put into the cast of *Blood Feast*. That terrible, terrible little movie which we shot in four and a half days for $24,500 in 35mm color, established a whole new genre of film. It was years ahead of *Friday the 13th*, *Texas Chainsaw Massacre*, *Halloween* — the first real slasher/gore film. It stood alone for a good ten years before someone really tried something like it again.

*The late David Friedman poses in front of a poster for* Two Thousand Maniacs!

**Had you seen any other truly bloody movies before this one? The Europeans had experimented with it a little bit.**

Before *Blood Feast* I never saw blood in color. I think this was probably the first picture where people even died with their eyes open. I was a movie freak; I'd been going to the movies forever and ever, and I've always loved action pictures. If somebody got shot, you didn't see gushing blood. The guy clutched his chest and closed his eyes and fell down. Nobody ever made anything like John Woo, where he slaughters five thousand people in one reel! It's funny, he uses a gun for most of 'em. I grant you, a submachine gun can put a lot of lead in somebody, but he didn't use anything really horrible like an icepick or a machete.

A lot of the idea for *Blood Feast* came from comic books.

**Like the E.C. Comics.**

Yeah. There was that psychiatrist, Wertham, who wrote the book *Seduction of the Innocent*. He ranted and raved about comics leading children into spasms of violence. He had close ups of eye injury, things like that. Outside of that Bunuel film [*Un Chien Andalou*] with the razor and the eyeball, you never saw anything that extreme, even in the few Oriental films that came in. Once in a while you would see some jungle footage of animals tearing one another apart, but I don't recall any human mutilation prior to *Blood Feast*.

So, for better or for worse, this is what it did. There was a great review in *Variety*: "The fact that it takes itself seriously makes it all the more deplorable." I wrote back to the reviewer, "Whoever said we were taking it seriously?" We were laughing all the time, and the biggest chore was trying hard to keep those girls from giggling while they were being "mutilated."

So gore, blood, slasher — that became an exploitation field. We had a lot of imitators, like *The Undertaker and His Pals*, that came along a few years later, but as far as major distribution, it wasn't until Sean Cunningham's *Friday the 13th* that you saw that on a mainstream scale.

**The Europeans had a kind of give and take with that, too.**

Not to sound grandiose here, but I think *Blood Feast* may have inspired some of the Italians. Mario Bava, for example, and Jesus Franco. Those fellows didn't do anything that extreme prior to *Blood Feast*.

**It's interesting that Bava did one major horror movie before that, Black Sunday, but it was so heavily censored in the U.S. You guys got yours out totally uncut, with blood flying everywhere, while that film was two years earlier, with about 10 seconds of gore cut out.**

Yeah, it took a while for America to really get on the bandwagon. All the violence today has become gunfire, though some of the effects are absolutely astounding, starting with *American Werewolf in London* and things like that. Herschell has always said we should make *Blood Feast 2*, but there's no way in the world we could compete. We're still thinking in terms like, boy, if we had $100,000, what kind of picture could we make? You tell that to anybody in Hollywood and they'll kick you out of the door. What are you gonna do, make a trailer?

**You could maybe feed the cast and crew for a day.**

Yeah! Now, most of *Blood Feast* was just pure showmanship. Vomit bags and all that. I would go into towns and swear out an injunction to get the film from being played in the town. In Sarasota, Florida, the injunction stuck, and I couldn't get it lifted! Then you have the manager of the theater make sure that any children who come unaccompanied by an adult had a letter from their parents. In Tampa, we opened the picture at a downtown theater, and about six hundred kids showed up, all of them with a letter. Of course, 90 percent of them, they'd written the letters themselves! Those were the fun things.

I kind of feel sorry for a lot of guys in the exploitation film business today, making these pictures that go straight to home video and maybe cable. Guys like Fred Olen Ray, Jim Wynorski — the Friedman and Lewises of the nineties. They'll never have the thrill of standing in front of a theater, watching people come in and walk out in various stages of disgust or shock. That was the joy of the business, not necessarily making the things but getting them distributed and standing to watch 'em as they came out.

**The last movie I can think of that really follows that tradition is** Basket Case.

Frank Henenlotter, yeah. That whole idea goes back to show business where there was a black woman, Mary Lou William, who actually had the torso of her twin growing out of her chest. That was not a medical impossibility, with the twin being attached. Of course Mary Lou kept the body of the twin as her livelihood, but that premise wasn't too farfetched for us carnival guys.

Good picture, by the way.

**I'll never forget them handing out those surgical masks at the theater doors.**

They had some great-looking freaks in the third *Basket Case*, where they kept them all in this house. Of course, nothing ever topped the first one — nothing ever does, really. I know Frank really well; talk about a walking encyclopedia of exploitation, that's Frank.

**Now you followed up** Blood Feast **with** Two Thousand Maniacs.

That was really Herschell's. I had been in New York and seen *Brigadoon*, so when I came back I was telling Herschell this story of a little Scottish town that came to life every hundred years. Herschell was always fascinated with everything Southern, although he was Chicago born and educated — supremely educated, I might add. He had taught English at Southern

Mississippi, and I think we got along so well because he thought I was another Southern redneck . . . which I am! Out of that he came up with a Southern town that was massacred by the Yankees, so it comes to life every hundred years and gets revenge. I went down to Florida to search for locations and came up with this little town, St. Cloud, which is where Disneyworld is today. They bought land down there for a hundred dollars an acre while we were making the picture. There was an old hotel in the front of the town, and we spent about eight days there, shooting that film. That one was a lot of fun. It had a pretty fair story and a hell of a soundtrack!

*"Yee-Haw!"*

"The South's Gonna Rise Again!" Somebody even put out an album of that. I was out in L.A. And met a young man I'd been talking to for a long, long time. He was interested in making a picture about Russ Meyer's life story or my life story, so I went over for a little meeting with these fellas. They said, "We'd like to remake *Two Thousand Maniacs*." I said, "Well, I think I can see what you've got in mind — 1901 to 2001." They kind of laughed and said yeah. But then they've gotta figure out what happened in 1901 other than McKinley getting shot! That was a Polish anarchist, so you couldn't really blame Southerners for that. So I said I'd look through my history books and find out some terrible thing that happened in 1901 that somebody might want to avenge years later.

***You could always make something up, some Yankee mass murderer.***

Sure! The amazing thing to me is that, as junky as these pictures were, they've continued to live all these years, even before there was such a thing as video. These pictures played every drive-in theater in the South, to be played at least once a year. There came a point that *Blood Feast* and *Two Thousand Maniacs* became the same thing and had to be shown. They were like perennials, the flowers. Then when video came out, there weren't too many distributors. I didn't think there would even be a market for it.

***But there was!***

Oh, yeah. About a dozen companies have put it out as the rights would change from one place to another. Just the theatrical releasing of the damn things always amazed me, even up into the eighties these were still playing.

***So what will the Something Weird editions be like?***

They're absolutely perfect, from the original negatives. I don't have a DVD machine, but now I'll have to get one!

***What other titles can we expect?***

There's the whole "Blood Trilogy," obviously, that Herschell and I made together. *Color Me Blood Red* is the third film in the trilogy, about a mad artist who finds out blood is just the hidden pigment he was looking for.

All three films were shot in Florida. At that time, Herschell and I both lived in Chicago, and I owned and operated a fairly successful independent film distributing organization there. Herschell came in one day and said he was going to make a picture, and I said, well, take a number. Then he said, "You don't understand. I've got all the financing." I said, "Well, sit down, please!" And he made a picture called *The Prime Time* — Karen Black's first movie, which she was in for all of about fifteen seconds, when she was a student at Northwestern — and followed it with *Living Venus*, which starred a young Harvey Korman.

After those two, Herschell and I started making nudie cuties. I'd known Russ Meyer and seen his first picture [*The Immoral Mr. Teas*]. We were very successful, and every exhibitor with an adult theater at the time wanted to make his own picture. They would hire Herschell and me to make them; we must have done thirty of them. Then we thought about what we could do that nobody else had ever done, something in extremely bad taste.

I'd do anything to get out of Chicago in the winter, so we made one of the early nudist camp pictures, *Daughter of the Sun*, down in Florida. It was Herschell's first trip there, and he fell in love with it. From then on, all we would do every winter was plan to make four or five pictures in and around Miami, which we did. We shot *Blood Feast* in Miami, *Two Thousand Maniacs* in St. Cloud, and *Color Me Blood Red* in Sarasota, where I'd spend most of my winters anyway. Those pictures were our great excuse to get out of Chicago and spend several weeks in Florida making pictures — a nice bonus.

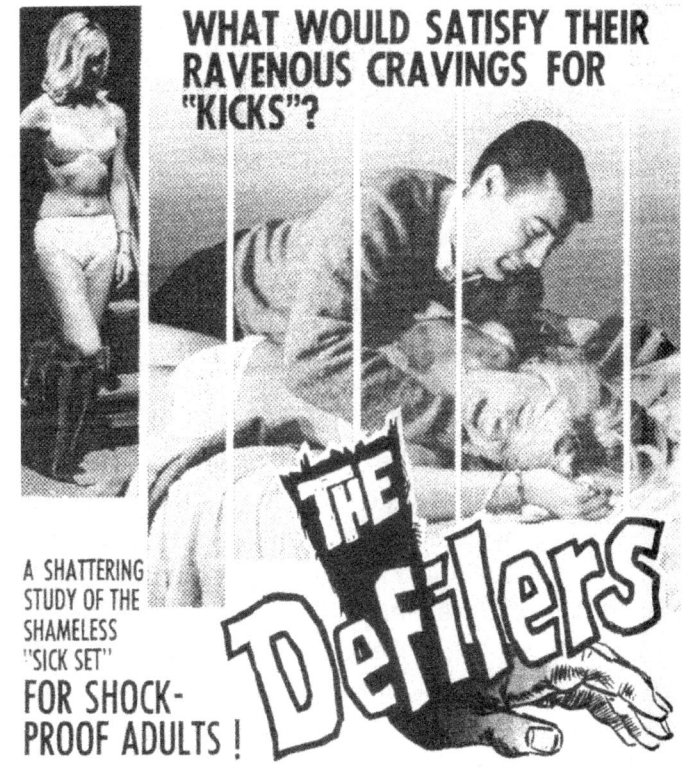

*In the "Blood Trilogy" it's interesting how much the actual amount of blood seems to get smaller as the movies go on. Color Me Blood Red is much more story-driven, with only one really graphic scene.*

Yeah, where the guts are hanging out. I can't answer that one. I think it just happened that way. In *Two Thousand Maniacs*, the executions were not quite as graphic as the ones in *Blood Feast*. The scene on the beach where Fuad rips the girl's head open and scoops out her brains, or where he's flogging the girl to death, and so on. In *Two Thousand Maniacs*, the barrel roll and the rock didn't lend themselves to the amount of blood we had used before. It wasn't anything planned, just happenstance. We had found this cosmetic company in Miami that had developed this stage blood with the viscosity of human blood, and it also photographed like a million dollars. It also could be swallowed without causing too much bodily harm.

***Too much?***

Well, we never told the actors, but the chemist who sold it to us kind of laughed when I asked whether we could put it in people's mouths. He said, "Yeah, but I gotta tell ya, one of the ingredients is Kaopectate."

A great scene in *Blood Feast* is the one where I'm drunk and taking the girl up the stairs in the motel. When I go back to get more whiskey, Fuad comes in and forces her down on the bed, then rips her tongue out. This girl had a large mouth, which was how we happened to cast her. Her name was Astrid Olsen. I found her at a Playboy Club one night. We filled her mouth with strawberry gelatin as blood, so she's looking up at the camera and all that's in this gaping cave of a mouth is this gurgling cauldron of strawberry jam and fake blood.

Later on, one of the only pictures I didn't put my name on was *Ilsa, She-Wolf of the SS*, made for a bunch of Canadians. It was a very sad experience; these Canadian guys couldn't have gotten a phone installed in Los Angeles. I had just finished a picture at the old Selznick lot, *The Erotic Adventures of Zorro*, and so I was well known on that lot. The old *Hogan's Heroes* set was on the backlot there, and I knew that they had sold that property for condominiums. I asked the studio manager if I could burn that thing down, and he said sure, do anything you want. So I made this picture for these Canadians, and it was a mess. I hired this young make-up guy named Joe Blasco, and he got into it. He came up with some of the greatest effects I've ever seen. Later on he became the head of make-up at ABC and runs a series of schools on make-up. He came up with all those effects, and they worked like gangbusters. Of course that was a relatively bigger budget picture, $110,000. It was at the same studio where *Gone with the Wind* was made!

**Ilsa's *another movie that refuses to die.***

They really played a money game on that one; the money was coming to Panama, Luxembourg, Nova Scotia, then to Los Angeles. I never had any money. Every day I'd need money, and it wasn't at the bank. They'd call and say it should be there. One day I needed $50,000 to pay off everybody, and they said, "Could you lend us $50,000 for a couple of days?" I said, "I'm working for you — what is this?"

They wouldn't have been able to step foot across the border of the United States if they'd gone through with that. So the money finally showed up. I made the rough cut in L.A. And sent it up to Montreal. They sent it back with notes like "Reel 1, 12 ft, 6 frames, take out 1 frame." I said, "What are you talking about? This is a rough assembly, not the finished cut. Why don't you finish it up there, take my name off of it, and send me my check?" Don Edmonds, whom I'd hired to direct the thing, went on to do a couple more for him, which weren't that bloody. I had known Dyanne Thorne from burlesque; she really loved that part.

**You could tell! There's a lesser known movie of yours that's really excellent, A Smell of Honey, a Swallow of Brine. How do you feel about that one now?**

I love that picture. I had found Barbara Jean—Stacey Walker's the name I gave her — when we were getting ready to make *The Notorious Daughter of Fanny Hill*. We'd gone out to Santa Monica one day to have lunch, walking along the beach, and this girl comes up to ask if we'd give her a dollar for a hot dog. We got to talking with her, and she was a runaway from Texas. The more I looked at her, she had a real Texas twang in her voice, but she was gorgeous. I said, "How would you like to be in a movie?" She said, [heavy twang] "Aw, you kiddin'!" "I'm not kidding. What are you talking about? Play Fanny Hill. She's supposed to be an English courtesan." Who the hell's going to be listening to her? They're gonna be looking at her. So we put her in this picture, and Laszlo Kovacs shot it. In fact, he shot *Smell of Honey*, too.

While we were shooting this, I thought I'd better get something going for this kid right away before my competitors grabbed ahold of her. So I wrote *Smell of Honey*. The original title was *The Maneater*, but I knew no newspaper would take that. By that time these long, tricky titles were in vogue; Radley Metzger was using *Soft Skin on Black Silk*, that kind of thing. It became *A Smell of Honey, a Swallow of Brine* — she leads them on and yells rape. The interesting thing in that picture is the scene where the guy is having a dream sequence, where he's tied up and she's whipping him, then she's tied up and he's whipping her. That kid was named Sam Melville, just a young actor looking for work in L.A. About six months later he got into a series called *The Rookies*, about three young cops, and that thing ran for a long time. I showed my friend A.C. Lyles a rough cut of the film, and he said, "Bring this girl over to me at Paramount. I wanna talk to her." The day I was supposed to pick her up, she'd cut out and gone back to Texas. She was a nutcase, but boy, she was beautiful.

**That's too bad. She was great in that movie.**

She was very good in *Fanny Hill*, too. The only other thing she made was a short I did at a nudist camp out in San Bernadino, called *But Charlie, I Never Played Volleyball*. We shot the whole thing in one afternoon. You can get it through Something Weird.

**I've never seen that one!**

I liked that little picture. It cost about $11,000 to make. It was fun to make, with all practical locations.

**We probably won't see that one on DVD soon, but at least it's on tape.**

Some of the DVDs will be great. We're doing *Erotic Adventures of Zorro*, and we're doing *Space Thing*. There's "the picture that makes *Plan 9 from Outer Space* look like *Citizen Kane*."

**Yeah, but yours is in color.**

Then there's *The Adult Story of Jekyll & Hyde*, and the two Betty Page pictures.

**How did [Russ Meyer regular] Stuart Lancaster wind up doing Long Swift Sword of Siegfried and all those other films with you?**

He did *Lustful Turk* and *Starlet*, too. I got him through Russ. He's a grandson of the Ringlings and at one point was Vice-President of Ringling Bros. Barnum & Bailey, so I'd known him in Sarasota. He was one of the elite there, and he took his first inheritance and invested it in a little theater there. When Johnny North got control of the circus, he ousted the rest of the family, who were called the 49ers because they had 49 percent while Johnny had 51. They had to stand aside while he ran the show.

Stuart's theater went belly-up, so he came out to Hollywood and found work with Russ. When he got his second inheritance, Russ advised him on that, and I think he saved some money. The last time I was in L.A., I asked Russ to go see Stuart, but he's in the hospital. I had shot *Siegfried* in Germany and dubbed it at Paramount, so Stuart became one of the voices there. He was great in *Starlet*, a good little picture. The story of Entertainment Ventures, Inc. We shot that at the old Monogram Studios before it became a radio station. The same thing with *Trader Hornee*.

**That's one of the most visually beautiful movies you've done — great eye candy.**

All those exteriors were shot at the Franklin Canyon Reservoir about five minutes north of the Beverly Hills Hotel! All the black people were from South Central. For that scene with the big entrance with the elephant, the cameraman called me over and said, "Look up there. There's some guy way up there looking down at us with binoculars from a five million dollar house." Here are all these black people and an elephant, and this one guy was so funny — standing there in his outrageous costume, he said, "I think I'm gonna walk up there and knock on his door and say, 'Hey, man, we're your new neighbors!'"

# Frank Henenlotter
## by Colleen Wanglund

**EDITOR'S NOTE:** Frank Henenlotter made his feature directorial debut with the cult film *Basket Case*. He has since directed two *Basket Case* sequels, as well as *Brain Damage*, *Frankenhooker*, and *Bad Biology*. In 2011, he co-directed a documentary (with Jimmy Maslon) on Herschell Gordon Lewis entitled *Herschell Gordon Lewis: The Godfather of Gore*.

On September 27, 2011, the cult classic *Basket Case*, about the weird relationship between two brothers, finally comes to Blu-ray. Lovingly restored and supervised by director Frank Henenlotter himself, the new Blu-ray bosts the film's best version since it was filmed.

I recently had the chance to talk with Frank, who tried to avoid a film career and yet is one of the most popular independent grindhouse filmmakers since Herschell Gordon Lewis.

*How did you get your start making films?*

I just made them. I took my father's 8mm camera and I graduated to a 16mm camera. I just loved making movies. I never intended them to be commercial. In fact, I never intended them to be seen; I just enjoyed making movies. I never intended to have a career out of it, and I still don't think I want one out of it. I don't think I've had a career. . . I'm just a guy who's made a couple of movies.

*Who or what were some of your early influences?*

The biggest influence on me was 42nd St. (Times Square, NYC) in the 1970s and '80s. You could see everything there . . . you could see just everything, and it wasn't just about the exploitation stuff; horror one day, sexploitation another, an action film this day, a cult film over here, women-in-prison films — oh, God, I love those! — it was everything. It was the perfect film school.

**Yeah, I miss the old Times Square.**

Miss it, it's criminal what they've done. It looks like a shopping mall now. It has none of the flavor it used to. I felt totally at home there. I used to cut high school when I was 15 years old, and I would go there and for all those years I never saw any problems. I didn't see the crime, I didn't see anything. I didn't have any trouble. I loved it. I just loved it. When I finally moved to Manhattan I would be there six nights a week. It was my element. I also enjoyed the seediness of it all . . . the fact that between the theaters were porno stores. What started first as just adult book stores eventually mutated into something else.

I loved it, and I always had an excuse to go into the shops. "Well, the film doesn't start for another ten minutes, so maybe I can just, oh, wander around this book store for a minute?" And you stare at as many covers as you can, you feel good and then you go see a horror movie. I mean, what's more enjoyable than that? Now, because I loved film so much I would occasionally sneak off to the repertory houses to see a bunch of Hollywood classics. You need that yin and yang; you need both to keep your stomach from getting upset. But it was mostly the exploitation stuff that I just reveled in.

**I've heard about a movie you made called Slash of the Knife. Can you tell me a bit about it?**

*Slash of the Knife* was just one of many oddball

movies I had made. It was twenty minutes long. It was the first time I had done 16mm with sound and I just thought it would be fun to do a phony documentary that looked like it was made in 1952 like one of those sex hygiene movies. So I did the phony sex hygiene documentary on the joys of circumcision. I just thought it was the stupidest thing to make a movie about, and we played it absolutely serious, and everyone was just shaking their heads because I don't think anybody but I got the joke, but everybody liked the fact that it was crackpot and ridiculous.

**I hope we get to see it eventually.**

Probably not, but it's okay because I recycled the two best jokes from that in *Bad Biology* (2008).

**Where did the idea for Basket Case come from? What was the inspiration for the story?**

The title and nothing more than that. When I was making *Slash of the Knife*, I met Edgar Ievins who was making a plasticine baby at the time for a scene at the end of it, and he was just watching and he said, "You ever think about doing one commercially?" And I said, "Yeah, I mean, we could, it's not a big deal." Edgar said he could get the money, and he did get some money, and that's what we did it on. We also thought if we shoot a horror film we have to show it on 42nd St. and I was very comfortable with that. When I was making *Basket Case*, I thought I was making a film that would never be seen — except for being shown on 42nd St. I thought we'd make it real fast and make our money back. I didn't think I was making a film I'd have to live with the rest of my life!

**And yet there are so many fans of it. It's a huge cult classic.**

I know, but that was not in my mind. You don't set out saying, "I think I'm gonna make a cult movie that'll last 40 years." My concern was just finishing the damn thing. We wanted to do a horror film, but I didn't have any ideas. I was playing with horror movie titles in my head. I was doing, like, "Lunatic," "Crazy House," this or that. And then I came up with *Basket Case* and immediately got this ridiculous visual of a young man walking around with basically a malignant jack-in-the-box, and I thought the idea was so funny. And I thought, "Wow, it could be at a skid row hotel and this and that." What I didn't know was, and I couldn't lick this for the longest time, why would anyone walk around with a monster in a basket? I was just about at the point where I was thinking, "Well, I don't know, maybe this isn't that good an idea."

I was sitting in Nathan's in Times Square, eating a hot dog, and it just occurred to me. "What if it's his brother in the basket? That's a great idea." And then the whole thing just flowed from there, you know what I mean?

The script just suddenly wrote itself, and it was like, boom, done. And I thought it would come and go, and that was fine with me.

I was so caught off guard that the distribution company who bought the film, Analysis Films, didn't sell it on 42nd St. but instead opened it as a midnight movie, which back then in the '80s was for crackpot, underground, demented films. Not like what's seen at midnight today. That's how they sold it, and that's what happened. For two-and-a-half years it was playing midnights at the Waverly Theater (now the IFC Center), which is only a couple of blocks away from where I live. I'd see the people lining up for *Basket Case* and shake my head in wonder because I couldn't understand why these people would go see it.

**They liked it!**

I know they liked it, but I still don't know why. I mean, I'm not complaining — far from it — but I don't have an explanation for its popularity.

**Well, as a fan I can tell you it's funny, it's gory, and it's just a great movie to watch.**

If that's what it is, I'll take it. That's all a film needs to be actually, entertainment.

**How long did it take you to go from first draft on the script to completed film?**

Well, shooting the film was dragged out over a year because we didn't have the money. It was horrible. There were weeks when the film I shot was still in the lab because we didn't have any money to pull it out. We couldn't look at it, so it was pretty terrible. Whenever we'd get a little bit of money, we'd see who was around and see if we could keep going. My goal under those circumstances was just completing the thing. That became the issue—how many more shots do I need before I can sign off on this? So it was not a fun way of making it. The filmmaking was fun to do but just not having the money wasn't.

**How did you find Kevin Van Hentenryck?**

Kevin and the entire cast were found by Ilze Balodis. Remember the scene where there's a social worker with glasses and high hair — puffed up hair? By the way, she did that hairdo just to make me laugh because she knew every time I'd look at her I couldn't stop laughing. That was Ilze, and she did all the casting for the film. She worked for the Brooklyn Academy of Dramatic Arts, and that's where she knew Kevin and virtually everyone else in the film. She was the one who got me the entire cast of the movie. That's why they were good and they got the joke. They knew what they were doing. We shot it for $35,000 so not only didn't they get paid, but we could barely afford the lab costs to get the stuff developed. So they knew what they were in for. But they didn't care — they were just there having a good time with it all.

**For the love of film . . .**

Yeah, and hoping to God that maybe the asshole director knew what he was doing, so they could start a resume, you know?

**Well, it turns out the director knew what he was doing.**

Well, I don't know about that. I'm sure some of them have very good resumes and *Basket Case* is probably not on there.

**What is different about this new release of Basket Case compared to Something Weird's previous DVD release in 2001?**

A couple of things. First of all, just doing it in high definition makes a hell of a difference because it's the closest we could do to having a 35mm image in your home. It's that stunning. But in this case, this is the first time I actually sat in on the transfer of a film and babied it. Also, I had all the elements. Since I did the DVD I found the original 16mm negative. It wasn't complete, but we had enough . . . about 80 percent of it. We also found the 16mm release print. It was missing only one reel but we have it, so when I brought it to the lab I also had the 35mm interpositive (an orange-based film with a postive image made from the edited camera negative) print. We did a comparison on everything. We compared the

*A scene from Frank Henenlotter's film,* Brain Damage.

16mm to the IP. They were virtually identical which was good because it was easier to work from the 35mm IP, but we kept the 16mm reels there for reference. Anytime there was a question about how a scene should look, we'd go back to the 16mm.

What I tried to do, and because of HD was able to do, was make the film look like the 16mm movie that I shot. Not the film which was theatrically released, which was a disaster in terms of how it turned out. When it was theatrically released, the 35mm prints had a bad duplicate negative made and they were all way too dark, all flat color. They just looked awful. And I remember when I was shooting the film I always thought *Basket Case* was bright and colorful, which are two words you could not use to describe it seeing it in the theater. So I wanted to restore it to the version the public never saw but the distributors did because we had to 16mm prints that we would show distributors, and they looked bright and colorful and looked wonderful. I remember at the end of editing it I wished I had done something a little different for the night scenes. So I asked the lab if we could add a very subtle blue tint to most of the night scenes, and oh, I loved it. It looked great. It came out looking really good. But it was lost when we did the blow-ups, because it wasn't built into the negative. So all of that I was able to go back and put into this. Compared to the DVD it's cleaner, brighter, and nighttime has the right tint. I just think it looks great. Like I've said, if you keep polishing that turd, one of these days it'll glow. It'll still be a turd, but it'll glow fine. And I think we finally have that little turd glowing now.

**What was the process like to transfer the 16mm negative to high definition? How long did it take?**

The actual work on it only took about two weeks, but getting there took a while. It was finding the lab, looking at the material, and getting them to agree to do it with me there, and it was quite lengthy. It was funny, too, because one of the guys at the lab looked it up online and all of a sudden was like, "Oh, this film's got a good reputation. We're going to do this one right!" And I'm thinking, "Thank you! Thank you!" I was very happy with it. It all worked out. Right now I don't know how I could improve on the film even more, and I still left a lot of it alone. I left everything that was in the negative there. If there was a hair in the gate (during projection), I left it in. I didn't care since it was there from day one. I just cleaned up all the problems that were accumulated on top of it all.

**So it still has that gritty look to it.**

Oh, it always will. I just don't want it to be dark and ugly. It'll be a little brighter. The DVD was brighter than the VHS and I never heard anybody complain. I never heard anybody say to me, "Oh, I wish it was darker and depressing like the VHS."

**With both Basket Case and Brain Damage you managed to do horror/comedy and yet both Duane and Brian are tragic figures. How difficult is it to write such tragedy without taking the story in too dark and somber direction?**

I don't know. That's a balancing act that's fun. Part of what I enjoy is not being one or the other. I'm not a big fan of straight horror movies. I think they're kind of boring. But to give you a horror film that has a twist or something interesting or a little perverse dark humor, I'm there. I love that stuff. And I'm talking about films like the original *Texas Chainsaw Massacre*. There are scenes in that film that are hysterically funny and they were meant to be. So that's what I'm talking about; and the original *Psycho*. Once you know Norman's story, you watch that film and realize, "Oh, my God, they're doing jokes!" So I found that balancing act fun. You know, comedy is in everything. I just like that mix of it, that's all. The only one I didn't do that with was *Frankenhooker*. I really wanted that to be a straight-out comedy. That's why I didn't put any blood or gore in that one.

**I laughed my ass off during that one.**

Well, there you go. I don't think you would have laughed as much if there was blood and gore in it. I think if those hookers had blown up spurting blood it wouldn't be funny. Now it's like fireworks and it's one of the funniest scenes I've ever done. It's my favorite scene out of all my movies. I see it now and I just go hysterical laughing over it. I can watch hookers explode all day long.

**As far as the two sequels, Basket Case 2 is a good movie. However, Basket Case 3: The Progeny is a train wreck. What happened?**

Well, it's a long story. Part three is a disaster and it's all my fault. I can't blame anybody else. It shouldn't have been made. It's as simple as that. BC2 I'm very happy with because I was able to come up with something different. I didn't want to do a sequel that was a rehash of the first one. I didn't want them going to another fleabag hotel . . . "Oh, you forgot to kill additional doctors . . . " I didn't want that. So I thought the idea of having a community of freaks was pretty exciting. What I really shouldn't have done . . . I shouldn't have done part three until I had a radical new idea. So that's that, you know? It's a film that I will be embarrassed of my whole life because I actually made that one (laughing).

**I guess shit happens, right?**

Yeah, and you know, having said that, I loved the experience of making it, no problem with it. I'm thankful I had the chance to make it. It didn't come out the way I wanted, but so what?

**Brain Damage has a sort of Trojan horse message about how bad drug use is. Was it done intentionally?**

Oh, absolutely. One of my problems in that one was, "Okay, I take the *Basket Case* idea of a monster leaping out at you but instead of leaping out of a basket it leaps off a guy's body. Okay, why would anyone intentionally want a parasite living on their body?" It's been done a thousand times in science fiction films where they're bitten and lose will power. So I thought, "Well, I don't know. What if it's something a little more complex than that?" And I immediately thought of Elmer injecting him (Brian) with drugs and I thought, "Oh, wow, that's great. Let him be the voice of cocaine," which is a drug I understood back then that damned near killed me. Every time I wrote Elmer that was like my old bottles of cocaine calling to me, you know what I mean? So I thought that made sense. I think it was a great metaphor for the movie. It's a little unusual, you know? Yeah, I'm very happy with that one.

**You have avoided Hollywood throughout your career. Why is that?**
I avoided a career. I would have never fit in, in Hollywood. I just would not have fit in. I'm just not interested in those kinds of movies. I would have to clean up my act so much. I would have to compromise so much. There's no Hollywood studio that would have said yes to the scripts I did. Simple as that. Why go there and pretend to be something else? Yeah, for the money, but eh, I don't know I just didn't want to make movies bad enough, especially after *BC3* — to start making movies I really didn't want to make. Nothing more than that. And then for 16 years I didn't even want to make movies.

**Now that leads me to another point. I read in a previous interview where you say with movies, mainstream and commercial are two different things. How so?**
*Basket Case* was very commercial but not mainstream because it made money. All commercial has to be is a hook that makes money for the theater so it gets sold. Look at how many mainstream movies have been made since 1981 that are forgotten about now. And this wretched little movie of mine is still selling. That was my point. And the reason is maybe because those movies were too much like other mainstream movies — safe and predictable. What separates them from thousands of other ones, really nothing. On the other hand, there are not too many like *Basket Case*, and thank God for that (laughing). You know, you say, "What the hell is wrong with this film?" No, what's right with this film — it still makes money.

**With the apparent lack of imagination in Hollywood right now and all the remakes it's cranking out, how would you feel if someone wanted to do a big budget remake of any of your films?**
Oh, I stopped seeing Hollywood movies years ago. It's the same movie over and over and over again. That's not what the genre is. They already have come to me about it. The only way I'm going to do it is if they pay me so much money that I have to go along with it. But that hasn't happened

yet. I wouldn't mind selling out. Honest to God, I'd be happy to sell out. I mean, I have a price tag like everybody else does. I wouldn't participate in the remake but, you know, I have a price tag. I've recently had people flirt with a remake of *Basket Case*, but I haven't inked the deal. I'm not anxious for a remake. I think that's the ultimate sell-out. I also think it isn't an easy film for them to remake because it doesn't fit into the slasher category. They probably have to make Belial legs, you know? And then he carries a machete and wears a mask.

# Jack Hill
## by Chris Watson

Jack Hill was born in Los Angeles in 1933, the son of an art director for Disney and Warner Bros. Hill studied film at UCLA, where he was classmates with Francis Ford Coppola. While at UCLA, Hill directed his first short film, *The Host*, which featured a young Sid Haig. He was given his big break in the film industry when he and Coppola were selected for internships with Roger Corman on the 1963 thriller *The Terror*, starring Boris Karloff. Corman immediately recognized potential in Hill, and as a result, the would-be director was promoted to screenwriter. Hill then wrote additional scenes for and served as second unit director on Coppola's debut film *Dementia 13*.

Hill, who would ultimately be recognized as one of the greatest exploitation filmmakers of all time, soon began writing and directing his own projects for Corman. He would ultimately direct nearly 20 feature films. Among them are the blaxploitation classics *The Big Doll House*, *The Big Bird Cage*, *Coffy*, and *Foxy Brown*. These films are significant because they established Pam Grier as a true star and also because they are generally regarded as some of the best films of the blaxploitation cycle.

*You've said there was a lot of racism in the film industry at the time these films were being made. What was the attitude of the studios toward these films?*

I can only speak for the studio I was working for, which was AIP. Well, I got a taste of it from some other people, too. The people in production at the studios had contempt for all of these movies they were making — not just for blaxploitation.

Here's a good example. After *Coffy* came out, I was talking to other companies and producers about doing films. Here I had just made a movie that was like the number 12 grosser of the year on an extremely low budget, but all people would say was, "Aw, that was a black film. That doesn't count." And I talked to a producer who was interested in making a black film, and it was kind of a mystery to him as far as what worked in black films. He said, "I know they like to laugh, and I know the picture shouldn't be too good." I did not have further conversation with him on the subject.

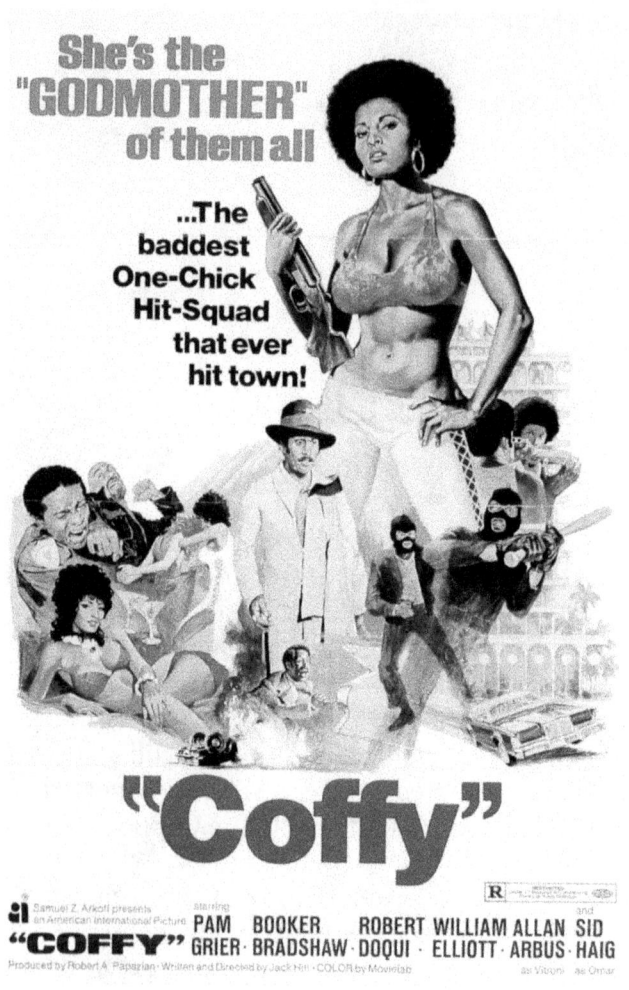

**Did critics treat blaxploitation films differently?**

Yeah. You have to read some of the reviews of the time. One described Pam Grier as "an unsympathetic black chick." One of them said "black tart." They used that kind of language that you would never use if they were, say, Jewish. "Jewish tart." You would never say that. Not if you knew what was good for you. And the reviewers treated them as junk films.

And now those films are all analyzed by sociologists and treated by critics as classics. People are finding all kinds of messages there. I was recently interviewed by a girl who was a college professor in Birmingham in England. She teaches *Coffy* in her course on black American culture. Writing a book on the subject — that would have been absolutely unthinkable back in the 1970s.

*You made several films with Roger Corman. What was Corman like as a producer?*

Well, it was like a split thing. On the one hand, he would give you lots of freedom once he'd approved what you were doing. He could do this because he knew as a director himself that the way to get the best results from you was to just leave you alone. He would not interfere unless you were going completely off the rails, and then he knew he could take over himself if he needed to. So he could take chances on people. Because he knew if something went wrong, he could just step in and fix it himself. Most of the people you would work for wouldn't have that capability or that confidence. So that was what was great about it.

The bad thing about it was that he would have mood swings. Sometimes he would come in in the mornings and there was like a black cloud over his head. He would turn purple and kind of give you all kinds of wacky orders that people would just ignore. And of course, he was just terribly cheap with money. He would sign contracts that he had no intention of keeping.

But you got to make movies.

*So what were some of the budgets and shooting schedules like?*

Quite often Roger wouldn't even bother to have a budget. He just tried to do it as cheaply as he could. He really wasn't that interested in taking the time to make budgets. He left that to you. Basically he just wanted to make everything as cheap as possible.

*Sometimes budgetary restrictions force you to make artistic choices that actually benefit the films. Did you find instances of that?*

Quite often. When you don't have money to do things, you have to come up with other ideas. And sometimes you are forced to come up with ideas that are very, very good. And the good thing about Roger Corman was that he wasn't like a lot of these people who would read the script and then you'd have to have two lawyers to sign off on it if you wanted to change a single line. And that does happen. Roger quite often wouldn't even read the script. He would read the first draft and tell you to change this or that, and then he would just assume you would do it. And then you go out and shoot. If you wanted to make up something on the spot, that would be fine by him. That's kind of rare. [Laughs.] But it certainly is a great way to work. Unfortunately you can get into the habit of working that way and then you go to work for people who don't do that. It can be very tough and make you feel very restrained.

Roger was all for getting a maximum effect with a minimum of means. So working with him was excellent training.

**Were there ever any extra challenges being a white director making what is considered a black film?**

No. That never occurred to me at the time at all. The unfortunate thing in regards to racism . . . at the time I started doing these pictures for AIP, the studio was very, very conscious of criticism in the media about not having black people behind the camera. But when we made *Coffy*, we searched everywhere, and there simply were no qualified black technicians available. For one thing, it was a union film. And to get into the union . . . it was very difficult to get into the union and you had to have years and years of experience. And often you had to be the son of somebody who was already in — forget the daughter; women working in the industry were almost as rare as black people. But I hope the success of those films — with a general audience, not solely a black audience — contributed to the acceptance by audiences of black characters and black lifestyles in films. And it gradually brought black characters and black lifestyles into mainstream films. And now you rarely see a film without black or Hispanic actors in prominent roles. So if I made any contribution in making that happen, I am very pleased about it.

**Pam Grier's character in The Big Doll House was originally written for a white woman. Is that right?**

Well, it didn't specify, and if it didn't specify, then you assume that it is, so yeah. I interviewed all kinds of actresses, just people who were strong. I didn't restrict it to white or anything else. I interviewed Pam. She just came in in kind of a cattle call. I was looking for an ensemble, so I would have groups of girls come in and read in groups so I could see how they played off each other. And the first time I saw Pam, I was really struck by the presence and authority she had, even though she hardly had any experience at all. I don't know if she'd had any training. I didn't even ask. She just struck me right off as being such a powerful personality that I felt she'd be right for the movie. And she was.

**What was she like to work with from a director's standpoint?**

She was great. She was thoroughly professional. She prepared very thoroughly. She was just totally professional in every way, and she learned very rapidly. Sid Haig helped her a lot as an actress. They had quite a few scenes together. So all I can say is that it was a very happy relationship all the way around.

**What inspired you to cast Sid and Pam as lovers in The Big Bird Cage?**

I cast them because I thought they had worked so well together in *The Big Doll House*, and basically almost stole the show. Sid, of course, was someone I had worked with almost from the beginning. I liked to write roles for him. I just felt they were a good couple. You know, chemistry. They have chemistry.

***Your films often feature women in positions of power. Is that a theme that interests you personally, or was this just by chance?***

Both. It just kind of happened that way because that was the assignment. And once you got a reputation for something, that's what everyone wants you to do. But also, I enjoyed it. I was looking for something a little bit different to do. Also, I always felt that actresses loved to play those types of roles, so that kind of makes it fun for everybody involved. And as it turned out, audiences liked it also.

***You once joked, "I plead guilty to racism," referring to Coffy. What did you mean by that?***

I never said that. There's a lot of misquoting in this business. Unless it was reverse racism. A lot of people accused *Coffy* and *Foxy Brown* of being racism in reverse. I might have said something like that. [Laughs.] Because it was fun. I was never trying to send any kind of message, or make any kind of statement. Everything I did was just what I thought made a good yarn — good drama. It's been pointed out that not only are all the bad people [in these films] white, but they're also men. That's not entirely true, but people have said that. Maybe it just seems that way because the normal run of films before that were different.

The great thing about the blaxploitation movement, if I may use that term, is that . . . you see, the civil rights movement put a lot of black actors and actresses out of work. Because before that, they were playing mostly maids and servants, comic relief like Stepin Fetchit and things like that. So the studios didn't want to do that. They didn't want to put people in demeaning roles, but they didn't really know what else to do with them. So blaxploitation opened up a whole field for black actors to play in. So if someone was supposed to play a pimp, he didn't find that demeaning at all. "Can you play a pimp?" "Boy, can I play a pimp." That was the attitude. Whether they thought it was demeaning at that time, I don't know. But they certainly never indicated that to me. Maybe in hindsight they might look back and feel that way, but it was a way to get started. They were really happy to have those roles at the time. Especially Robert DoQui, who played King George in *Coffy*. He told me he was so happy. For years after that, he said people would come up to him on the street and say, "Hey, King George!" He was famous for playing a pimp, and he loved it. Because it was a good role. It had a lot of size to it.

***You once observed that most black actors who were involved with these films look upon them with great fondness, yet many of the white actors now look upon them with disdain. What are your thoughts on this?***

Who can figure actors? Actors were very, very happy to get the job at the time. Then they suddenly change their minds after a few years,

especially if they got successful with something else. That was the reaction in those days. But after 30 years — now that the pictures are acclaimed as classics and people like you are interviewing us — they suddenly change their feelings about it. Like Peter Brown, who was very happy to get the job in *Foxy Brown* at the time. I saw him a couple years later, and he didn't remember who I was, and he referred to the film in some really, really demeaning way. And then 20 years after that, I ran into him at a convention where he was signing autographs on a picture of him and Pam Grier. And it turned out that that was what he was best known for. So he changed his feeling. Like I said, who can figure actors?

***Foxy Brown** was originally supposed to be a sequel to **Coffy**, and was initially titled* Burn, Coffy, Burn. *What factors led to this being changed?*

The studio sales department declared that they didn't want any more sequels, and somebody in that department came up with the title *Foxy Brown*. And a star was born! I think it was a mistake. I think we should have had a franchise. And the head of production, Larry Gordon, who was always very supportive of me, felt that way, too. But the sales department had the last word in cases like that. I think it was stupid. At least I thought it was stupid at the time. But as it turns out, *Foxy Brown* — maybe it's the title, which is so far over the top — has become the more popular film. I suspect that's the reason for its popularity. [Laughs.]

*Which of these films is your favorite?*

I don't really have any favorites. I think that *Coffy* is, in many ways, just a really, really good piece of work. I'm really proud of it. Unfortunately, it had to be done on such a low budget. I think it could have been really good had we more money to spend. It was a good script and a good story. We had a great cast, and it was just well done in spite of its handicaps and limitations. And that's the one that people who study these things tend to find the most entertaining, as well. And I can tell you that the audience reaction to it was almost frightening. People would stand up and yell at the screen. It was quite thrilling! [Laughs.]

**A projectionist told me that the theaters had to have security when they would show blaxploitation movies. He said that if the audience saw whites or Mexicans working in the theater, they would throw stuff at them.**

I never heard that. I did hear one time that a lot of theaters stopped showing the films because there was too much damage to the theaters. [Chuckles.] I never saw any of that at the screenings I went to. That's catharsis, I think they call it. There was a real participation by the audience in the action on screen. They talked back to the actors and yelled at the characters on the screen.

I don't know how it got started, but it may have been a custom that began in the black churches, where they respond to the person who's giving the sermon. That could be where they got into that kind of habit. But I did see that with *The Big Doll House*, too, and that was not a primarily black audience. People talked back to the characters. That's a phenomenon. One critic mentioned in his review when *Coffy* was playing in the drive-in theaters that people would honk their horns at various places in the film. I never saw that happen, but it makes sense.

**You've said that you wrote some stuff in Foxy Brown simply to spite AIP. Is that right?**

I would hate to use the word spite. Well, you could use that word. [Laughs.] I didn't like the way they were treating me. I did put some things in it because of the studio. I think maybe because *Coffy* was such a big hit, they were afraid I was gonna run wild or something. They really tightened up on things. So basically I got so disgusted with it that I threw things in with the idea that they would say no, that was going too far. [Chuckles.] But they bought it.

You know, it was only at the last minute that they invited me back to make a sequel. There were reasons they didn't want to work with me. Actually, what happened was that they had invited me to a screening of a movie they were very proud of. And I walked out of it, very foolishly. And they swore I would never work then again. But with *Coffy*, which was one of the biggest hits they ever had, I think Sam Arkoff overruled the other guys. But they invited me back to do the sequel at the last minute, so to speak. So I didn't have time to work out the sequel as well as I had with *Coffy*. I just tried to throw in everything over the top and have fun with it.

*Are you ever surprised by the impact that those films have had on popular culture?*

Yeah. At the time, most of the films I made were expected to play one summer — maybe two summers if they were a hit — and then be forgotten. It was only after the advent of home video and the revival of the films that the whole attitude towards them changed. Yeah, I was surprised. I mean, you never set out to make a cult movie. There was no such thing at that time. Basically I was given an assignment to do a certain type of movie, and I just did the best I could with it. I never treated any of my assignments lightly. I always tried to do something better than what anyone would expect. And most of the films were commercially successful at the time, and some of them were major hits. But the idea of them being studied by sociologists 20 years later was certainly never in anyone's mind. [Laughs.]

*To what would you credit the resurgence of these films?*

I think people today are able to find things in the films that they are missing in films today. Everything today is made from fear. Everything is just a clone of something else. At least until recently, when there's been a kind of revival in independent filmmaking, where people can go out with some videotape and make their own film. But the mainstream industry is just trying to play it safe. So these films have a certain kind of vigor and insolence, which is maybe a characteristic of my films. Impudence. People find them very refreshing and exciting.

# Alejandro Jodorowsky
## by Andrew Leavold

A temple priest shits into a glass bowl and it turns into gold. A cowboy rides past a river of blood from a hundred murdered brides. An armless dwarf, a legless midget, a sea of Christs and a skinned goat crucifixion.

Profane, disturbing, infuriating, inspired: the world of Chilean-born mystic artist and filmmaker Alejandro Jodorowsky (or, in his words, the "Jodo Multi-Universe") is a multi-tiered journey into the furthest reaches of human experience, be it real, hyper-real or otherwise. His two most characteristically perverse works have been mostly out of circulation since their releases; now *El Topo* and *The Holy Mountain*, films as enigmatic as their creator, are restored to the Dendy George Street screen courtesy of IMA in pristine, restruck 35mm prints.

Via e-mail from Paris, his home since his "Mexican phase," Jodorowsky speculates on the filmmaker as shaman, film as alchemic trigger, and his role as creator of an incredible new Multi-Universe.

*When I saw* El Topo *and* Holy Mountain *at age 20, I was affected the most by the potent images and baffled by the non-linear narrative. Now at 38 I'm looking for symbols and ideas behind those symbols. In 20 years time I will no doubt see something else. Is this not what art is meant to be — ambiguous, timeless, multi-layered, designed to provoke and infuriate as well as inspire?*

Yes. I always tried to create images with many interpretation levels. Every spectator in front of one of my images can have a different reaction. Laugh, cry, get mad, love and hate. But the unique thing I am looking for as a unique reaction of the audience is when they look at the picture, even if they don't understand it completely, they will never forget it.

*I haven't seen the remastered version of* Holy Mountain, *but the new print of* El Topo *looks absolutely stunning — the colours! The clarity! Just how much time and effort went into perfecting the new prints of* Fando and Liz, El Topo, *and* The Holy Mountain?

I remastered the three pictures in only one week in New York. I could do that because I had an amazing technical crew. Allen Klein invested in this remasterization $500,000. May he be blessed.

*You were quoted in the sixties as saying, "We are not; we are becoming." This is alchemical, is it not? How would you describe this philosophy to those who have never heard of alchemy or other esoteric systems? And how can films — like psychedelics, like meditation — trigger the alchemical idea of transmutation?*

A still from the Alejandro Jodorowsky film, El Topo.

The whole alchemy can be summed up in one sentence: "the spiritualization of the matter and at the same time the materialization of the spirit." In the Christian symbology Jesus Christ represents the materialization of the spirit and Virgin Mary the spiritualization of the matter. Through meditation, this process happens in ourselves. Our mental learns to drive its material life to realization and in the same time our body learns to integrate the spirit. Here's what my movies are containing.

*I find this interesting: souls are eternal and interdimensional, and yet are trapped in these eating, shitting, fornicating, procreating, and ultimately decaying and dying three-dimensional biological machines. Some people crave the mystical experience and yet react strongly to or reject depictions of such primal things as blood, conflict, sexuality, death, putrefecation, and even bodily imperfection. Why do you think there is such an unbroachable divide between the spiritual and the carnal for many?*

For more than 2,000 years religion has divided our being in body and soul as if they were separated. It is the matter of the universe that is producing conscience. We are the song of the stone. Christ, the Virgin Mary, and the 12 apostles, same as Buddha and Mahomet, have produced each in his life no less than six tons of shit.

**Jung's influence on both your art and your work in psychoanalysis is strong, but there are also echoes of Wilhelm Reich. Which of his theories appealed to you and why?**

I like Reich in his theory of "Orgone." A sexual energy, which fills the atmosphere. Which is in fact only the "Prana" of Hindu mysticism. The healing virtue of the orgasm is a genius idea.

*A scene from Alejandro Jodorowsky's film,* Holy Mountain.

**Fando and Lis *and* El Topo *both appear to be heavily influenced from your work with Teatro Panico. Theatre and cinema are not dissimilar but the two are still different languages. How did you go about translating your stage experience into films?***

I don't translate experience. I inspired myself of schizophrenic people. I can be a lot of characters. The theatrical director is not the movie-maker, not the poet, not the mime, not the therapist, etc. I believe that every man can be multiple, like for example Leonardo da Vinci or Jean Cocteau.

**The Holy Mountain *is the closest you have come to making a science fiction film. If you had made* Dune, *how would you describe it now? And if you had no budgetary restrictions, what kind of science fiction film would you make?***

If you want to know this, read my two comic books — *The Incal* and *The Metabarons*.

**Like Bunuel, your Mexican films resemble no other films made in Mexico. You both have an outsider's perspective on its unique landscape and iconography. As someone born outside of Mexican culture, what were you able to draw from this unique experience?**

Each bottle of wine has a different taste according to where the grapes are grown. The Burgundy is different from Beaujolais but none of them are superior to one another.

**In the second part of Holy Mountain, in which you are introduced as a Master, the intricate overhead shots — showing the table at the center of the eye, and the tiny figures walking around huge symbols — are incredible. I understand you were working with a substantially bigger budget than El Topo, but I can only imagine how much preparation and execution went into the entire movie! Just how complicated did the Holy Mountain shoot become, and how satisfied were you with the results?**

In reality, at this time I demanded to the movie to be as profound as a sacred text, an evangle, or a sutra. I wanted a cinema able to change the human being, illuminating him. I didn't use actors. In this movie a millionaire is a millionaire, a whore is a whore, a Nazi is a Nazi, a degenerate is a degenerate, a shaman is a real shaman. I filmed 35 hours in incredible circumstances where we risked our lives. For example we all jumped in the middle of the Caribbean Sea where there are sharks. Why we did this? For me the ocean was the symbol of the mystery. I wanted us to get free of the rational prison to full enter in the deep dark waters of the unconscious. We all almost drown. The technical crew instead of film saved us. The two hours duration of the Holy Mountain are only a trace of an essential mystical and missed experience. I wanted to illuminate the people I filmed. Instead of making holy monks I made amateur actors ready to prostitute themselves in the industry.

**In Tarot I've always been interested in the Hanged Man, a card which I believe is a signal of potential transformation. This theme is throughout El Topo and Holy Mountain, as is (I suspect) a great deal of Tarot-inspired imagery. What is your interpretation of the Hanged Man?**

*A photograph from the Alejandro Jodorowsky film,* Holy Mountain.

The Hanged Man cut himself from the world to find his real inner-self.

I spent a great deal of time working in the Philippines, filming a documentary about their famous midget James Bond called Weng Weng. In their culture, dwarves and midgets are revered as special and almost holy, as if blessed by God, and not cursed or feared.

**What is your instinctual belief and the source of your fascination with using their images?**

I love all that is not mediocre and reveals imagination. The monsters are for me forms of biological art. They are a special form of beauty. Hieronymous Bosch understood that, Brugel, Goya, Velasquez, Picasso, all the surrealists, and in cinema Todd Browning, Bunuel, Fellini, Guillermo del Toro, and many others. When I was a kid — 8 years old — my favorite hero was the Frankenstein monster.

**What are your feelings these days about your lesser-known films Tusk and The Rainbow Thief?**

I don't like them. When I shot those two pictures, I was in misery and needed to feed my family. I was obliged to make concessions.

**You described the world (or worlds) you create as Jodo universe. What form does Jodo Universe take these days?**

Now it is not a Jodo universe, but a Jodo multi-universe.

# Lloyd Kaufman
## by David Carroll and Kyla Ward

**EDITOR'S NOTE:** Lloyd Kaufman and Michael Herz established Troma Films in 1976. The two have since co-directed more than 30 films, including *The Toxic Avenger, Class of Nuke 'Em High*, and *Sgt. Kabukiman, NYPD*. Kaufman has also produced nearly 100 titles, including *Mother's Day, Slaughter Party,* and the documentary *Make Your Own Damn Movie!*.

*It was a cold night in Sydney. We had left the Japanese restaurant early to catch* Sgt. Kabukiman NYPD *at the Valhalla Cinema. We met Lloyd Kaufman and said, "Do you ever get up on a bad morning and want to make another Apocalypse Now?" He said, "No, I just want to keep exploding heads."*

*We never saw him again. But we did catch up with him over the phone a week or two later, at his New York home. He said he was distracted after a day's shooting, but proved an enthusiastic and obliging subject for an interview. One gets the feeling he really takes public relations very seriously.*

*And now, Mr. Kaufman talks about life, movies, and philosophy — Troma style.*

**Firstly, I was wondering if you could just tell us a bit about your background, and where it all started?**

Well, Michael Herz and I went to Yale University, and we were infected with the movie fever, and we saw such great movies as Chaplin, and Keaton, and John Ford westerns, and we decided we wanted to make movies outside the studio system and try to give what we had to give to the movie-going public.

*This was obviously long before video; were there any differences in going to movies back then? Has video changed it a lot?*

Well, you know, 1994 will be Troma's 20th anniversary; and originally we made our movies for the movie theaters — for the cinemas — and we really are still making our movies for the cinemas. Video has come in and has democratized the movie industry quite a bit; it has made many movies accessible to the public, and it has made the public accessible to many independent film makers.

*Is it easier to make movies now that you can put them out on video?*

Well, the biggest problem, and I think we all have the same problem, is that the communication industry has become so consolidated, and has become so merged; and everything is done on such a giant scale that there are very very few independent movie studios left. In a way it is much more difficult for an independent movie director, or an independent movie studio, to get its movies to the public, because the game has become so much more expensive. Troma, which is a movie studio, has to compete against Time-Warner, which owns TV stations, cable television networks, broadcast TV stations, *Time* magazine, and Warner Brothers Studios and book p ublishing, and its music empire.

Our little movie company which only makes movies has to compete against that, whereas 20 years ago, there were quite a number of small, independent movie studios all surviving nicely in and around the major Hollywood studios, before those major Hollywood studios became such giant international communication conglomerates.

*Is it a problem with distribution, or getting the money, or what?*

Well, I don't know how it is in Australia, but in America the average movie now costs $25 million dollars, American, to produce, and then another $10 to $15 million dollars to market. And that is an awful lot of money. Twenty years ago that was not the case. Twenty years ago a movie could open in New York City, which is certainly one of the more important cities in America, and you could be the biggest movie in town for about fifty thousand dollars U.S. You could be, in terms of advertising, the big movie. And now, if you're going to open a movie in New York and you want to be the big movie for that week, you're talking about $800,000. So clearly, what Troma has to do, and what Troma has always done, is to provide the adventure in movie going.

The reason that Troma has survived, and just about every other American independent studio has died, is that the public who go to the Troma movies in the cinemas go — not because of the huge advertising budget, or big stars, or the fact that we are part of a giant conglomerate — they go because of the Troma brand name. Troma has a brand name, which means an adventure in movie watching. The person who goes to the Troma movie knows that he or she may love the Troma movie or, he or she may hate the Troma movie; but the movie goer knows that he or she will never forget the Troma movie. That's really what we give to the public — a movie like *The Toxic Avenger* or *The Class of Nuke 'em High* or *Class of Nuke 'em High Part III: The Good, the Bad and the Subhumanoid*, or *Sgt. Kabukiman NYPD*; these are all very high-concept Troma movies which are very unforgettable and totally different from anything that the big Hollywood conglomerates are giving to the public.

**In the beginning, did you have the idea of that sort of style, or did you just get into movies any way you could?**

Well, I love movies, period, and it just so happens, as Shakespeare said, "to thine own self be true." The kinds of scripts that I tend to write are Tromatic, and so we tended to be involved in these rather unusual projects like *The Toxic Avenger*, which basically came out of the newspapers. Most of the scripts we write, and most of the movies that we produce in-house, have their roots in the newspapers; they come out of newspaper stories. *Sgt. Kabukiman NYPD* came from the newspapers; one of the big stories is that United States and Japan are having a great conflict now for the economic and cultural supremacy of the world, yet they love each other and Sgt. Kabukiman is a symbol for that. Sgt. Kabukiman originally was a New York City policeman who loves hotdogs and beer, and through a quirk of fate he transforms into a strange-looking kabuki actor with super powers, and you know it's a very crazy movie but it has a basis in fact. *Class of Nuke 'em High*, which has gone on to two sequels, revolves around the fact that nuclear power plants are built in a shoddy, corrupt manner; also a newspaper story that we read about in 1986.

*You've said a couple of times in interviews I've read that Roger Corman has influenced you. He was obviously very successful at making low budget movies.*

Well, when I was at college, and I had to make the decision — do I go into one of the giant movie studios and play that game, or, would it be possible to go against all the odds and try to make my own movies in low budget? Is it possible to make good quality low budget movies? The only example that we could find was Roger Corman — he was doing it! This is in the late sixties I'm talking about; I saw wonderful movies written and/or directed by Roger Corman — well produced, well written, beautifully acted, and rather provocative. And that was proof that indeed, good movies could be made on a low budget. That was enough for me and I decided there was no reason why I could not go off on my own and create low budget movies that would be good! And hopefully Troma has done that. The public has responded for 20 years, and Roger Corman is one of our role models.

*And he's still going, as well.*

He sure is! He's a very good friend.

*You mentioned the smaller companies having troubles at the moment with the conglomerates. There have been a lot of really successful movies recently that have not come out of the Hollywood system. Is it changing, the conception of small movie makers?*

I think that for every Crying Game, or for every The Piano, or for every Enchanted April, the battlefield is littered with hundreds of wonderful movies that have gotten destroyed by the fact that they simply could not get decent distribution, by virtue of the fact the cartel is very very difficult to crack.

Troma's been lucky because we have a Troma universe, we've got a brand name, and people see that Troma logo on a movie and they go see it because they know what they're going to get. We have fans that we've built up over 20 years; people collect our posters and movie stills — Tromabilia we call it. We actually have a mail-order catalogue and people collect it, and we've got a good solid base of fans. And every once in a while one of our movies like The Class of Nuke 'em High or The Toxic Avenger or, we think, Sgt. Kabukiman, become bigger, more mainstream hits than the typical Troma hit. In the case of the smaller movies produced by independent film-makers who do not have Troma's help, the only way for them to get attention, unfortunately, is to be slaves to the giant studios. Otherwise it is impossible for them to get their films out to the public.

*On to actual movie-making. You said a normal movie costs $25 million. What about a Troma movie?*

We're making movies now for between one million and three million. Sgt. Kabukiman NYPD cost about three million dollars U.S., and The Class of *Nuke 'em High Part III: The Good the Bad and the Subhumanoid* cost about $1.2 million. *Chopper Chicks in Zombie Town*, which is currently playing down-under, is about $800,000 U.S. But we have a brand new movie, which was directed by a wonderful, talented first-time director, called *Vegas in Space* and the whole budget was less than $200,000. We're fairly eclectic, however; I think the average now is about one-two million dollars.

*How long would that take to film?*

It depends on the movie. When Michael Herz and I direct we spend about six to seven weeks on the actual filming, and we shoot a lot of film; we burn a lot of celluloid. We use multiple cameras . . . two or three camera units and we're filming round the clock, seven days a week. We don't spare film. Again, one of the nice things about Troma is that we have been empowering new, young directors and they are shooting on smaller budgets than we are and they are more careful about how much film they use. *Def By Temptation* and *Vegas in Space*, those Troma movies by first-time directors, may move a little faster on the set.

*What's it like, making movies?*

Michael Herz and I love it! You know, we've been doing it for 20 years, and what's great is that if you look at all of our posters you'll see that it's all the Troma team. We try to gather a great ensemble, and everyone that is working with us just loves what he or she is doing. And since the actors are usually young, first-time actors — talented but new at it — everybody is absolutely committed to the project. The experience of making a Troma movie is something that everybody lives with forever. It's sort of like going to camp, or some kind of incredible bonding experience. It's very hard to describe but it's a great life-experience. And since all of our movies are comedic there's a great deal of improvisation. Talented young actors love working on Troma movies.

We are pretty well organized, because we have to be, and we spend a lot of time preparing our movies; usually two or three months rehearsing — we rehearse on videotape and go to locations to videotape again — so when we get to the actual shooting the celluloid we then throw everything away and are in a position, if we wish, to totally rewrite. But because we are so well prepared we can afford to improvise a lot.

Michael Herz and I co-direct, which is very unusual, and we've co-directed maybe twenty-some odd movies (with an emphasis on the odd). In the history of the movie industry there's only been one or two co-directing teams who have even co-directed one or two movies. Michael and I hold the world's record for number of movies co-directed, so that gives a certain flavor, a certain energy — and on top of that anyone else who's around, anyone on the set, is a director. Everybody is a director — it's the

Troma team — anyone who's got a joke, anyone who's got an idea; until the film actually goes in front of the lens, until it's exposed, anything goes. The Troma truck driver, the pizza delivery man, we let them *all* direct if they have something to say!

**You were in Australia recently for Troma 2000. Can you tell us about that?**

Columbia-Tristar is establishing the Troma brand name in Australia, and they have been showing four Troma movies in the cinemas — *Sgt. Kabukiman NYPD*, *Subhumanoid Meltdown: Class of Nuke 'em High Part II*, *The Good the Bad and the Subhumanoid: Class of Nuke 'em High Part III*, and *Chopper Chicks in Zombie Town*. Those four movies have been showing in about ten cities in Australia, and at the same time Columbia-Tristar have been launching each month one or two Troma titles on video.

**We could only think of six titles in the shops before the current influx, so there's not too many of them around. [Note: actually, once we got hold of the filmography we realized the problem wasn't quite as bad as we thought — but was still pretty bad.]**

I think it's a damn shame, because we have quite a good following in Australia. It's just been very, very difficult to get our movies to the Australian public. And now, for the first time, Columbia-Tristar is capitalizing on the Troma brand name — the fact that Troma movies are fun, they're enjoyable, they're good for couples, a guy and his gal can have a great evening going out to see a Troma movie, or renting a Troma movie. They're a lot of fun and that's the key. So Columbia-Tristar has been doing a great job getting the name out. In the United States Troma has about 150 movies, and many of the video shops in America have corners for Troma movies. I think Columbia-Tristar is carefully establishing the Troma brand name and is looking to set up Troma sections in video-stores all over Australia and New Zealand.

**Another aspect in getting to the public is censorship. Do you have a lot of trouble getting exactly what you want out there?**

Not in Australia. Australian censorship is fairly reasonable, at least for our movies. I don't think we've had too much trouble. We have trouble in the United States because the censorship board in the United States is a privately run organization funded by the giant cartels and, in our opinion, there is a double standard. It's called the MPAA classification board — the Motion Picture Association of America — and, in our opinion, they are much more stringent on the independent movie than they are on the giant-made movie, so as a result the movie that has all sorts of blood and violence featuring Bruce Willis will get through, where, for our movie they make us chop everything out. We have found that, while movies get censored, at least there is a level-playing field in Australia. It seems everyone is treated pretty fair there. We have no complaints.

*Are there any other countries which give you a lot of trouble, besides the United States?*

That's the worst, because they're unfair. There's a double standard; they treat the big-shots better than they treat the little-shots. It's a disgrace. When I began in the movie business there were 20, 30, 40, 50 small movie studios all making movies, and one of the reasons so many of them have gone out of business is that, in my opinion, the MPAA has disemboweled many good, commercial, independent movies. And they've obviously eliminated a lot of their commercial possibilities, and therefore emasculated their commercial viability.

We made what we consider our masterpiece, *Troma's War*, and the movie was entirely disemboweled by the MPAA, and we feel it was unfair. It ruined that movie. By the time *Troma's War* was shown in the theaters it was so chopped up that nobody could understand it. That has happened to so many movies along the way. We at Troma believe the MPAA is one of the reasons why so many of the independent movie studios have died.

**Two movies I saw recently which weren't particularly Troma-like were Stuff Stephanie in the Incinerator *and* Dead Dudes in the House. *Do you do a lot of this variation.***

Well, again, movies are art and the spirit of the movie depends on the creators. For example, a movie like *Def by Temptation* (that might be the best Troma movie ever, and Michael Herz and I had nothing to do with creating that movie), it was a very talented young new writer/director. *Stuff Stephanie in the Incinerator* was another whose movie was the first one. *Dead Dudes in the House* was by a very talented director who lives near New York city, and who is a Troma fan, and clearly was influenced by Troma but, as you point out, it is quite different from the typical Lloyd Kaufman/Michael Herz directed movie.

It's part of our mission to be Troma, the independent's independent studio. We are very proud of the fact that in the past few years we have empowered new directors to make movies, to get a shot at learning their craft and also we have given some new directors an opportunity to get their movies distributed. Movies like *Dead Dudes in the House* are not big enough or commercial enough for these giant conglomerates to distribute, yet they are worthy films, and the people who make them are worthy and talented, but they need a chance to get out there and then, hopefully, the writers and directors and actors will get an opportunity to take the next step up, to bigger and more mainstream projects. That's precisely what happened to the director of *Def By Temptation*.

*And Kevin Costner, I do believe.*

There you go, that's right. He had to start somewhere, and Troma is proud to be the owner of some wonderful early Kevin Costner; his first two movies, actually.

*You started in the horror side of movies when you saw an article called "Horror Movies are Dead."*

That's what gave us the idea to move into that, yes. Just the fact the experts were saying that horror was dead — we knew from film history that since the beginning the horror film was very viable, and wasn't going to go away. We figured, well, if people weren't going to make horror movies temporarily, maybe there's an open window we could jump into and make a film in that genre, so when the vogue comes back we'll be at the forefront, and that's how The Toxic Avenger came about.

*Was that in the early Eighties?*

As I recall, sure, we made The Toxic Avenger around 1982.

*What about horror in the 1990s?*

I don't know. The majors seem to be doing them. I can't tell you, I'm not really an expert. Most of what we do is comedy, and even though we deal with horror, and science fiction, and sex, and war, and all the different genres, whenever we treat them they're usually comedies. Movies like The Toxic Avenger are not really frightening, they are funny. They have elements of gore in them, and fear and monsters, but the end result is fun, not fear. So I'm not really an expert on the horror format. But I get the sense that it is a genre that has a very good following, and anyone who is able to make a truly scary movie is going to be successful.

*You do a lot of comic-book/action sort of movies. What would you say to allegations you followed a lot of their sexist attitudes?*

Well, anyone who has ever seen our movies would not say that. The only people who would suggest that Troma is sexist are people that have not seen the movies. But Toxie has a girlfriend who is much smarter than he is, she is the one who has the moral high ground. Toxie is always true to his gal and takes good care of his mom — he's definitely not sexist. *The Squeeze Play*, a movie we made in 1976 or '77, is about a woman softball team, and it was a big hit for us, made 10 years before *A League of their Own*. And yes, the women were very bright, and they were aggressive and they played sports, and they were upset because the men were running away every weekend to go out and play sports and be macho, and the women wanted to do it. That doesn't sound sexist to me. Yes, the women happen to wear bikinis from time to time, but so what? So do the men. Besides, the bikinis in our films make a social statement. The small costumes represent the dwindling of our natural resources. We must use fewer resources.

***And* Surf Nazis Must Die . . .**

Well, there's certainly nothing sexist in that one. The hero is a fat, 60 year old woman. The hero of the movie . . . it's certainly the farthest thing from being sexist as possible. If you want a sexist movie, I was on an airplane with my little daughters going from New York to Los Angeles and there was a movie called *Pretty Woman* which glamorized prostitution. I don't know what rating it was, but it was on an airplane for all the little children to see, and this was Cinderella as a prostitute. To me that seemed a little sexist, but I didn't notice anybody going after whatever giant multinational studio made that picture. None of the woman's groups, nobody laid a finger or fingernail on it.

*It's a pretty dreadful movie.*

It's a disgrace! And it was accessible to all the small children.

First of all, Troma movies are very uplifting. The prestigious American CinemaTech in Los Angeles is doing a 20th anniversary Troma retrospective in June; the National Film Theatre in London has done a retrospective; the San Sebastian Film Festival has done a Troma retrospective. We've had film festivals across the world . . . In fact, the Australian Film Institute did a Troma season not too long ago. But the point is, even if there is something objectionable, these are for the most part R-rated movies to which small children cannot possibly be exposed, and the Hollywood boys are making these movies with G and PG ratings which are more violent and more sex-filled and more evil than anything you can imagine. And of course the Government of the United States of America does things that are infinitely more horrendous than anything . . . The President, to get his ratings, bombed Iraq and killed eight civilians, for real. Any little child could see that on TV. The Attorney General of the United States of America, not too long ago, barged into a religious commune and incinerated, with tanks, 88 women and children in Waco, Texas. Troma's an amateur compared to what's done in real life, and compared to what the major studios do. We're amateurs in this.

But I think the people who react to Troma in a negative way, when you ask them have you seen a Troma movie, they invariably say "no."

**Do you see yourself as an escape from that sort of stuff?**

Oh, I don't know. I think we provide good entertainment. Good, fun, crazy movies with interesting themes. As I say, most of the themes of our movies come right out of the newspapers, so there's a rather provocative basis to them. And yes, our movies are sexy, and yes they are violent, and they have science fiction, and they got monsters, and they got horror, but they're fun. That's the key. They're a lot of fun.

A movie like *Die Hard*, with Bruce Willis, or *Under Siege* — these are pretty entertaining movies, but they take their violence pretty seriously. Our movies are good natured, tongue-in-cheek, and fun, and I think that is where our success has come. We have a following, and we get a lot of women. Women love our movies because they go with their date on Saturday evening and they have a lot of fun, and they see something they've never seen before. And even if they know they will like it, or they'll hate it, they know they'll never forget it. That's also an attraction. We have a movie, *A Nymphoid Barbarian in Dinosaur Hell*, that's the kind of movie that is very entertaining, and a lot of fun, and has some pretty good dinosaurs in it, and a fine young nymphoid, but some people say it's the kind of movie that's so bad that it's good. And they have fun. I think it's a great movie, I love it.

*Sgt. Kabukiman, NYPD*, it's a much bigger budget, a lot more mainstream, it's got the Troma flavor to it, but it's something that's quite unique.

**What can we expect in the near future from you?**

As I mentioned, we have *Vegas in Space*, which has been playing in Los Angeles for three months, and it's opening in Japan on the Ginza. *Vegas in Space* is the first space-travel musical with a transvestite cast, and it's a lot of fun. We are now developing *The Toxic Avenger Part IV: Mr Toxie Goes to Washington*. We have just written the first draft of *Tromeo and Juliet*, Troma's tribute to the bard. We have some new titles — a film from a new director called *Teenage Cat Girls in Heat*, a lovely comedy, very cute. We're good for about 10 new movies each year. Michael Herz and I will direct one or two of those, and the rest of them will be by fine, new, young talent. Oliver Stone worked for us, years ago on a couple of projects. And Costner, as I mentioned. There are all sorts of well-known people who have been in, and honed their craft in, Troma movies, and hopefully our new movies will bring you the giants of tomorrow.

# Herschell Gordon Lewis
## by Andrew L. Rausch

Dubbed "the Godfather of Gore," filmmaker Herschell Gordon Lewis is best known for horror classics such as *Two Thousand Maniacs, Color Me Blood Red, A Taste of Blood,* and *Blood Feast,* with which he single-handedly invented the subgenre of the gore horror film. While movies such as *The Texas Chainsaw Massacre* and *Halloween* certainly owe a huge debt to Lewis, his influence has hardly been confined to horror. "Lewis is the man who put red meat into the American cinematic diet," film writer Joe Bob Briggs explains. "Ultimately, Herschell made Quentin Tarantino possible." Director John Waters, who has always been vocal regarding Lewis' influence on his own work (even going so far as to incorporate footage of *Blood Feast* into his own *Serial Mom*), takes this declaration a step further. "Without [Lewis] you wouldn't have *Jurassic Park*," he observed. "You wouldn't have any of these films where gore is accepted."

Despite Lewis' reputation as a master of terror, he also directed films in a number of other genres: family films (*Jimmy the Boy Wonder*), sexploitation (*Suburban Roulette*), and even one of the earliest blaxploitation pictures (*Black Love*). After 1972's *The Gore Gore Girls*, Lewis walked away from the film industry, focusing instead on a career in marketing. Today Lewis is a respected marketing strategist who lectures around the country, consults for major companies like Barnes & Noble, writes for numerous publications, and is the author of nearly 30 books. (His seminal 1984 tome *Direct Mail Copy That Sells!* is currently in its 17th printing.)

After a 30 year hiatus, Lewis returned to the director's seat for the long-awaited sequel *Blood Feast 2: All U Can Eat*. At the time of this writing, Lewis was in preproduction on his 37th directorial effort, *Win, Lose or Die*.

**You were once quoted as saying, [I] pity anyone who regards filmmaking as an artform and spends money based on that immature philosophy." Could you elaborate?**

I object to the auteur attitude. I object to any public-be-damned attitude, whether it pertains to what we sometimes laughingly refer to as "fine art," music, or motion pictures. The purpose of a motion picture, in my opinion — especially a low-budget motion picture — is to compete for playing time. It's the low-budget producers who are constantly caterwauling about audiences' lack of understanding. What they're saying is that audiences don't understand *them*, and my position is that they've got this absolutely inside out. It's their function to understand the audience, and not the other way around. This idea that I am creating a work of fine art, and the public be damned if they don't understand it, is backwards. "If they can't come to my level, those poor saps, they deserve to miss out on what I have prepared for them!"

Look, if I prepare a gourmet feast of monkey brains for vegetarians, I deserve to go out of business because I have totally misread the people who are supposed to be my targets. And one area in which I've had good fortune in the motion picture business, perhaps because I've treated it like a business, is producing what an audience is looking for. Sure, if I'm making *Harry Potter* or *Shrek* and I have that kind of promotional power behind me, I know my movie's going to get opened. But if I'm making a movie that represents something where I'm trying to compete and I completely misread the audience, then I'm on a level with *Ishtar* or *Town & Country*.

Another factor I would like to point out is that almost invariably these pictures have confounding titles which have no intention of drawing people into the theater. That puzzles me, too.

**On several films you served as screenwriter, director, producer, composer, cinematographer, and special effects technician. Did this result more from necessity or from a conscious desire to personally control the quality of the product?**

Well, you have an interesting point there. Of course I wanted to control the product. I think that becomes important in exact ratio to budget, which was the overriding factor in almost every decision I made. There are many places where I would give almost anything for another take. In the movie we just finished, oh, what I would have given for a zoom lens! That seems like a nominal expenditure, but apparently it was beyond the budget. What I would have given to have been able to have ripped this thing open in a different way, but we couldn't do it.

I wanted the control, but the reason I would, for example, write the score for these pictures, which was a much more brutal job than directing a movie — any damned fool can direct a movie — was because I didn't want to pay someone else to do it. Here's a movie that cost under $100,000 to make, and a professional composer would want $80,000 to score it! That's nonsense. Proof of my posture that I didn't really want to be regarded that way was the number of times I did this under a pseudonym. Yeah, I am absolutely proud of the theme songs from *Two Thousand Maniacs*, *Suburban Roulette*, *The Girl, the Body, and the Pill*, and *Living Venus*. I'm proud of them because they're not *terrible* pieces of music.

**When you made films like Two Thousand Maniacs and Blood Feast, were you aware of how unconventional it was for a filmmaker to serve in so many capacities?**

It never entered my mind. I assumed that Cecil B. DeMille never did that, but so what? No, I had not surrounded myself with underlings. It was a non-issue. We were on the set and these things needed to be done. An example of this was *A Taste of Blood*. We needed someone with a "limey" accent and nobody could do it. We hired an actor who didn't show up. Because that was his only line, he was only being paid $25 or $30. He never showed up and I had to shoot the scene, so I put on a stocking cap and borrowed some hair from one of our long-haired crew people and I took that role. I thought nothing of it. I didn't use my name on that. It was simply a matter of getting the job done. I did things like carrying cable. So what?

On my first two films, on which we used union crews, there was very little I could do. "This is my job. You get your hands off of that." I felt that was foolish, too. Here were a whole bunch of guys standing around because the two people whose job it was were working at a slow pace. And you try to get an assistant cameraman to load a magazine at 5:25 in the afternoon! It cannot be done because at 5:30 we go into overtime and you get at least an extra hour, so the eye is on the clock. Well, my eye was on the clock, too. One of the little regulations I imposed on our pictures was that we shoot till we're done, so I was able to surround myself with people who loved making movies, people who loved the idea of looking at the dailies and saying, "Wow! I had a part in that!" They would say, "You want me to hold this or that on camera? Yeah, what the heck." That's increasingly hard to come by, although making movies today is light years easier than it was then. Among other things, we have film speed. Much of what I was shooting was ASA-125, which is now called ISO. On this new film, we used 250. That's 10 times as fast. And I'm looking at a TV monitor so I can tell if there's a microphone in the picture! It's easier than it was, which I like, I admit.

I like being a big shot as much as anybody else does, but I don't like having a half-finished picture and running out of money.

*Regarding the constant evolution of filmmaking, you once cited changes in the industry in the 1970s from when you first began making features in 1960 as being one of the reasons for your 1972 retirement. What were some of the most significant changes which most affected the exploitation market?*

Well, what happened was — and I suppose to some extent I should take responsibility for it — the major companies lost their virginity relative to audience shock. Until we came along, audience shock consisted of someone suddenly having a strange hand poke them on the shoulder or opening a door and then recoiling in horror. The dimension that we added was what you might call hyper-realism. And while we had that area to ourselves as outlaws in the business, theaters regarded the playing of our pictures not just as an adventure, but almost the kind of adventure that you have going over Niagara Falls in a barrel. If you succeed, you sign autographs for the rest of your life. If you don't, your heirs sign autographs.

When the major companies began to ask themselves how long this had been going on, they invaded that turf with the kind of equipment and effects that made it impossible for the independents to compete. The independents also had, for example, bare breasts to themselves for years and years. Once the major companies said, "There's really nothing wrong with a bare breast as long as we rate the picture accordingly," the independents were driven out of that little niche. And what they had to do was to go deeper into that particular gulch. When I saw what was happening with that element, I got out of that because I could see that there was just one direction in which those movies were going. In the case of the gore movies, I just felt I had run my course. The playing time was diminishing. If a theater could play one of my movies, which had Joe Glutz in it, or a Sam Peckinpah movie which had William Holden in it, which film would that theater play? I had no clout to say, "Hey, play this one and I'll give you that one, too." The time had come, and I felt I'd had a good run.

Who would have ever dreamed of this Renaissance which has taken place, where instead of an outlaw I've become a prophet?

# William Lustig
## by Devin Faraci

**EDITOR'S NOTE:** *Bronx-born director William Lustig got his start making porn films. He then began making exploitation films such as* Maniac, Vigilante, Maniac Cop, *and* Uncle Sam. *He has directed a number of other films, including two Maniac Cop sequels. He is also the CEO of Blue Underground, which specializes in the release of exploitation films on DVD and Blu-Ray.*

**You have an incredible cast in Vigilante. Can you talk about getting Robert Forster for the lead?**

We were in pre-production and had hired another actor but it came to a point where we realized we had made a mistake, and we were desperate to find another actor. A friend of mine in California, Frank Pesce, who is also in *Vigilante*, had run into Robert Forster at a local club on Sunset Boulevard. Next thing you know, he put me on the phone with Bob and we made a deal with his agent and he was on a plane and shooting in New York in a couple of weeks.

**One of the things that always struck me about Vigilante is that it's a really dark movie. Even for that time, when films about crime overrunning society were in vogue, Vigilante seems to be among the darkest and most nihilistic. Was that coming from a place where you were personally? Where did that tone come from?**

It's interesting because what I felt I was making was a potboiler, first and foremost. I guess what you're probably responding to are a lot of the events that lead to Robert Forster going after the bad guys.

*Yeah. The level of crime is so extreme.*

If you're making an urban retribution film, you kind of want to be more extreme. That's what I tried to do with *Vigilante*, to make it the kind of film that would be a catharsis. You want to create events that will really rile audiences up so they get excited when the bad guys get their comeuppance. You want them to be doing extreme dastardly acts in order to get the audience's blood boiling.

*You made this in '82 or '83 for an exploitation circuit that's very different from the distribution world today. How much were you trying to hit the key elements of the genre that began with* Death Wish, *which audiences expected, versus how much you were trying to stake your own territory?*

*Death Wish* of course is the granddaddy of this kind of picture. After *Death Wish* there were the European, mostly Italian-made, films inspired by *Death Wish*. What I tried to do was make an American [version of those films]. What I saw it as, stylistically, was an urban spaghetti western. That's how I viewed it musically, and with all of the set ups of the characters. Even the bad guys kind of look like they're Indians a little bit. The music is very much inspired by Ennio Morricone. That's where I was really going with the film to distinguish it from *Death Wish*.

*You worked on Death Wish, right?*

I was an apprentice editor on *Death Wish*. All I did was what's called syncing the dailies, which is where you marry the picture and the sound for the editor to begin editing the film.

*Before you got into directing quote-unquote legit pictures you directed porn. How did you make the transition from porn to straight movies? Was it easier back then to make that leap?*

Actually it was inevitable because when you were doing adult movies you were shooting them like regular movies. It wasn't like today where those movies were made on DV cams and are made in two days. Two days? They're made in an hour! But it was a lot different then; you were playing the films in theaters, you had stories, there was some modicum of acting and they weren't just gonzo films.

There were many people during that time who made the jump between adult and exploitation films. It was very common.

*You learned the tools of the trade there.*

Absolutely. Adult films were my film school. I was able to learn the equipment, you learn proficiency. You learn how to shoot quick, how to be proficient with your time, and you get the insight into the equipment you need to make low budget movies. First and foremost as a director you need to know how to tell a story, but second you need to have the knowledge of the tools to be able to pull it off. What the adult business did was it gave me the knowledge of the tools.

*And you don't have the ability to go over budget or shoot extra days in porn.*

You're really disciplined. It's because it was shot like real movies, there was a crew of up to 10 to 15 people — that's not huge but that's a real crew. That's why you don't see people coming out of adult movies these days and going into exploitation or anything, because they're just making these quickies and gonzo films.

*After that your first film was* Maniac. *Joe Spinell came to you with the idea for that, right?*

I met Joe when I was a production assistant on a movie called *The Seven Ups*. Joe and I really bonded because we had a mutual love of horror films. We began hanging out, going to 42nd Street together seeing the latest horror films that opened that week. I have memories of Joe calling me at 3 in the morning saying 'Let's go see the 3:30 show of *Hollywood Hillside Strangler.*' We would go to 42nd Street and we would be amongst Hillside Stranglers watching the movie. That was a great learning experience.

I started doing the adult movies, but with an eye towards doing horror films, and a horror film starring Joe Spinell. We began developing some scripts and trying to raise the money to do a horror film. Finally we got so frustrated because nobody would give us the money; I had saved up some money doing adult films. Joe decided to throw in his paycheck from *Cruising*, and my boyhood friend Andy Garroni and with $48,000 we went out and shot *Maniac*.

***I was told that the other writer on the picture, C.A. Rosenberg, is a woman.***
Yes.

***That's interesting and seems like something a lot of people don't know. This is one of the most extreme horror movies ever, and it was written by a woman! What did she bring to it?***
She wrote the first draft of the movie, which was written more like a conventional cops chasing a serial killer. There were a lot of police in it, there was a detective. Joe wanted Jason Miller, his friend, to play the part. When Jason Miller dropped out of the project we decided that instead of replacing him to eliminate the police and to focus on the killer. We made it this lean, straightforward serial killer movie from the point of view of the serial killer and not to deviate from it and never show the world outside of his world. It made it a more intense movie. Plus we amped up the violence in the film.

Actually, it was a result of a Screen Actor's Guild provision. We couldn't afford to go SAG, and SAG has an exclusion for X-rated movies. They didn't call them pornography, they call it X-rated. If I had submitted *Maniac* to the MPAA, it would have been X-rated. The idea was that we were making effectively an X-rated movie, so Joe Spinnell who was a prominent member of Screen Actor's Guild, didn't get fined by his union for being in the movie. And neither did any of the other actors who appeared in the film who were Screen Actor's Guild members.

***That's a nice work around.***
And it worked for the film creatively, because we could go with extreme violence.

***And that got the film some notoriety.***
Exactly. Things happen and you take advantage of it.

***Did the notoriety of* Maniac *help* Vigilante *get made?***
Not just the notoriety but the financial success. *Maniac* did well financially, and it made an impact in the foreign markets, so when we went to do *Vigilante* there was interest from distributors all over the world.

***Your background is as an exploitation filmmaker, but your legacy may be that of someone who preserves great and off-beat movies with Blue Underground. How did that happen for you?***
What happened is that in the nineties the world of making independent genre movies changed. It became corporatized. It became something less appealing and the films were being made almost like they were studio films, but they weren't studio films. There was a lot of oversight, a lot of meddling in the projects. When I was making films in the eighties it was complete freedom. Even if I was making a film for a company they basically gave you the money and you showed them the film a few months later.

*What happened? Why that change?*

I think what happened is that the independent companies started to emulate the studios in installing middle management. They didn't trust the filmmakers as they did in the 80s. And these companies all imploded because of it. They weren't making interesting movies, and they increased their overheads. Also, the owners of the companies became less involved in the films. They delegated it to people who just weren't film people, who didn't have a good sense of film.

What I'm trying to say is that it became a situation where I became disinterested. At the same time I started doing film restorations for laser disc, and I was enjoying it. I was meeting people and preserving films that were being neglected and it was just a lot of fun. Then along came DVD and there I was at the infancy of DVD and it was something that

immediately was successful, and I was making a good living at it and I never looked back. It wasn't a conscious decision — it wasn't like one day I had an epiphany. It was just something that happened.

**Then you went to start your own company, Blue Underground. Now you're focusing on truly underserved films, especially Italian movies.**

I've always had an affection for those films. That's why I jump at the opportunity to put out Argento and Fulci films, because those are films I love.

**Is it a competitive environment for you to be getting these Argentos for Blu-ray?**

Not at all, because I got them when these films were languishing. Their VHS rights had expired and no one was interested in these movies. In the mid-nineties I was snatching up the rights to them and I've been maintaining the terms with these movies. It would be very costly for another company to come in and start from scratch and put them out. Because I have a good relationship with the licensors I distribute them perpetually.

**We're living in a remake happy world. I've heard about the possibility of a Maniac remake.**

There's one in the works.

**What about Maniac Cop?**

One of the things I'm in California to do is discuss with Larry Cohen what we want to do with it. I'm going to discuss with him how we're going to go ahead with that.

**But that's something you definitely want to do.**

Yeah, but one of the problems is…what would make it interesting is if we could somehow get back the rights to the first three films so that if we do another one whoever we do it with we can bring all the projects into that one place. It's always more interesting as a franchise than it is a one off.

**Is there a chance of you directing again?**

Definitely. I'm looking at projects to do. Not Maniac Cop, but other things. And as Blue Underground is really up on its feet at this point I do have the time to be able to do other projects to direct.

**You had talked in the past about Blue Underground producing stuff.**

I don't think that's really possible in today's economy. I'm just not set up to do it. It's just not something I think is wise to get into right now.

**What about digital streaming — stuff like Netflix? Does that feel to you like the next frontier?**

I think digital holds a lot of potential, but it's still in a phase where people are trying to figure out what to do. I would say that it's a market which is in a flux, but eventually it's going to get sorted out. But it's still not fully worked out yet.

# Russ Meyer

## by Sandra Gin Yep and Mike Carroll

**EDITOR'S NOTE:** *Nicknamed "the King of the Nudies" and "the Fellini of the sex industry," Russ Meyer made his directorial debut with 1959's* The Immoral Mr. Teas, *the first sexploitation picture to earn more than a million dollars. In the mid-Sixties, Meyer established his style with the black-and-white films* Lorna, Mudhoney, Motor Psycho, *and* Faster, Pussycat! Kill! Kill!, *which is considered, by and large, his finest film. He scored huge hits with the films* Vixen! *and* Beyond the Valley of the Dolls. *Meyer passed away in 2004 at the age of 82.*

**We're dealing with, it seems to me, two extremes. On the one hand we have the people who are picketing their local 7-11s against Playboy and the adult entertainment bookstores and what have you. I first wanted to ask you, Russ, what do you think of these people?**

The people that are picketing? Well, they draw attention to them. The only thing I find negative about it is that they sometimes awaken the interest of sting operations by the FBI and so forth. I think the do-gooders finally got wise about how to deal with the so-called hardcore people. That is to arrest them in as many areas simultaneously as they could, which means that the hardcore producer then has to defend himself in more than one state. He can't use the same counsel, because he's got to have a counsel in every state. It becomes a war of attrition, I think.

It's been years since I had those kind of hassles, and I'm basking in the glow of Mr. Charles Keating, formerly of the Citizens for Decent Literature's present stance in regards to the Savings & Loan thing. He was a really aggressive porn buster, as it were, in Cincinnati. I defended my picture *Vixen!* in 1969, which was a very straightforward picture. It received a lot of very good box office and things of that nature, but we made the mistake of going into his backyard. We were defeated in every court in the state. Fortunately, Justice Berger would not, at that time, accept Keating's wish that we go to the Supreme Court and get a definitive answer as to what is pornography. The Supreme Court has always tried to push it aside so they wouldn't have to come up with some sort of definition, which they can't seem to come up with.

I think it's regrettable that people are denied the freedom of viewing and enjoying, just as others enjoy the freedom of worship. I don't think anyone should be able to dictate to an adult what he can be able to see.

*What about the issue of hiding behind the first amendment and staying in business in adult entertainment?*

Well, my experiences . . . at this time and place I don't have any difficulty with it. As I pointed out, this was back in 1969. And that same old chestnut was brought back to the surface. It's exactly what the first amendment was about — freedom of expression and things of that nature. The porn busters — the revilers — will do anything at all to try to deny others the right to see what they wish to see. Maybe they're terrified of their position . . . Maybe they are terrified that they will possibly be swept under, as it were, by this all-engulfing tide of evil, lust, and degradation.

***Well, it seems as if some of their following have. There are the Jim Bakers, the Jimmy Swaggarts, and we can go on and on.***

Yeah, I enjoy seeing Jessica Hahn. She handles herself pretty well. She's got a 900 number . . . She looks attractive. I think she had a tenure at Hugh Hefner's mansion.

I've a feeling that in the final analysis, freedom of expression will survive. Look at this Mapplethorpe thing where they were exonerated in the toughest city in America, which is Cincinnati, Ohio. They're a bunch of German-Catholic toughies — the backbone of the kind of people that really did represent Mr. Keating. It's such a nice thing to see Mr. Keating in a lot of grief. I must say he put me through a wringer. He really put me through a wringer. I was doing a picture at Fox, *Beyond the Valley of the Dolls*, and at the same time defending, with the help of a great attorney, Elmer Gertz. Every day I'd have a chamber of horrors message from my lawyer; "burn all the pictures, get rid of the posters." And I was concerned. This man Keating really wanted to get me into the iron hotel, as it were. Fortunately I was spared that.

***That's another big question people are thinking. They see Russ Meyer today and they think, "How has he survived, the 'King of the Nudies'?" What is your formula? How have you survived the porn busters?***

They just took kind of one solid whack at me and then walked away because they couldn't put me in the tank. So I did fine. And also at the time when I was more sorely beleaguered, I was working at $20^{th}$ Century Fox, which is a pretty respectable organization. In my book, I have letters from the Citizens for Decent Literature kind of putting Zanuck down for giving me a shot at that, kind of bringing the studio down to its knees. "His mouth should be washed out," all these kinds of things.

I've survived, I suppose, because of the very nature of my films. The best thing I could liken them to is sort of being like cartoons. I was influenced by Al Capp to a large degree in my early years.

***His comedic sense?***

Well, satires mostly, although the next film I hope to make will be a comedy. Most of the others have been kind of satirical mostly.

***You wouldn't classify your works in any way, shape, or form as pornography?***

Well, it depends on how you pronounce it. If you say, "pornography," see that's the power the porn busters have given it. They've made a very big thing out of it. But porno . . . That can be a very light thing. It offers entertainment. If someone chooses to make reference to my material as being porno, let 'em take their best shots. It's not gonna disturb me. I like the idea that I'm being accepted as being an original. Unique. The fact that the films increase in interest as the years go by.

On German television I now have 10 films playing during family hour. No cuts. I'm very strict about this — you may not cut my films. I made some mistakes early in the game. For example, Britain has the worst censorship in the world; really dreadful censorship. These are played at a time when young Hans is eating his noodles or wurst, and no violence. The pictures don't have any violence in them. They're uptight about violence. But sex is all right. Not hardcore—you can't have that sort of thing.

**How about this country? We're more uptight about sex than we are violence.**

Yeah.

**Can you expound on that a little bit? What are your views on that? Do you think it's hypocritical?**

Well, I like the sex to be kind of special. I like that business of saying, "That's obscene." It generates interest. I like those people to get up and come militant at my stuff. I did at the time. I enjoyed that. If they hadn't condemned it, hell, who would have cared? It's better to keep stirring up the pot a little bit. Where it's tough is, as I pointed out earlier, economically they're going against people who can ill afford to defend themselves in lots of courts in many different jurisdictions. I'm sure lots of your readership will say, "Well, good for them. I'm glad they're finally gonna get them." But there doesn't seem to be any kind of case history that relates so-called pornography to crime, or where people have been used and abused. Everybody who works in the so-called hardcore films — I know a couple of producers who make those — they're happy to do it. They make good money, and they feel they are offering a service.

**That's continually what I hear, over and over, whether they're the adult entertainment shop owners . . . They're saying, "We provide a service. We fulfill a need."**

Absolutely. That's more important than anything else. The service is to entertain. There are a lot of people who fantasize about having a relationship with some outrageously abundant lady, but because of their background or the financial aspect of where they live, or just the wherewithal or the knowledge on how to hit on someone properly for example, it doesn't come. But they can in their cubicle or their room or wherever it is. They can enjoy themselves and fantasize. What's wrong with that?

**Russ, how did you become so uninhibited? I mean, as I said, the hypocrisy in this country is that we're uptight about these kinds of things. But you have made a living, a good living.**

Oh, a great living. I've made an enormous living. [Laughs.] Simply because the films refuse to die. They go; they just go and go . . . Finland's playing them on television now. France soon will do the same. Italy is anxious. I've done a lot of film festivals, and I keep the same film boiling in the pot. And another generation looks upon these films. I just toured Remini, off the Adriatic Coast in Italy and showed the 12 films, and every night it's packed! And these people had never heard of me before, but there's some kind of current that takes place, and they hear about it in some way. And those people sit there. And of course they had a translation system there — they had made cassette tapes that translated what the people were saying. It's great to be so warmly accepted by a totally foreign audience.

*In this country, how are you revered, if at all?*

Well, a man followed me out of a hardware store today. "You're Russ Meyer. I understand you're writing a book? When is it gonna be ready? I understand it's gonna cost $138.50." I said, "Yes, it's gonna be 18 pounds in weight. It's gonna be three volumes, printed on 150 pound stock, with 2,400 outrageously abundant photographs." He said, "I must have that."

People recognize me. If I'm walking down a street in Bremen or Hamburg, they say, "Hey, Russ!" And it's flattering. And again, having films that you've made and you realize that there's still great interest, and many instances still growing in interest. It's like something an ex-partner of mine whom I worked with on *The Immoral Mr. Teas* said, "Mail order — it works while you sleep." It's the same thing. You've got it out there, and people are renting cassettes, buying cassettes. We just shipped 20 cassettes to a man in Burma.

*So you're saying the appetite is there?*

Enormous.

*Will these "porn wars," as we call them, will they be with us forever?*

Well, if they didn't stir it up, people might say, "What's so special about them?" You know, I wouldn't be surprised if they're keeping the pot boiling . . .not because they want to, but because of the political aspect —there's a lot of pressure on the so-called do-gooders to get all of this stuff stamped out, in spite of the fact that there's another segment of society that really enjoys it. That's the sad part, but it's gonna go on as it has gone on and on. There are certain things that are repulsive — like child pornography and the animal crap and all that. But that's pretty well out of it, as far as I know.

But I'm not that knowledgeable about it all. I'm not really fond of hardcore pornography on a personal level, but I'm not against it. I'm not fond of it because it doesn't turn me on. My sense of humor is outrageous — big bosoms, square jaws. I think more than anything else I try to generate laughter, and if I do portray sex it's done in a way that one might be trying to compete with the Olympics or something of that nature. If you were practicing sex in the way that I might present it you might end up in traction or something. It's purposefully put on that way, and I think a lot of that has to do with the success of my films. This was a jokey aspect.

*What do you classify as pornographic?*

To me it would have to be something that is highly objectionable like children being involved and being taken advantage of. That I would find to be repugnant. But consenting adults? No. I can't see in any way, shape, or form—in spite of the fact that in some of the cases the filmmakers have come up with some pretty bizarre acts, and I'm sure you know what I'm talking about. But you don't have to buy that cassette; if it has something to do with anal intercourse, you don't have to buy it. There are others that are more in line with what is conventional. Taste is in the beholder.

*To each their own? And in the privacy of their own home?*

Yeah, they're trying to . . . they've tried from time to time to intrude, you know. But it's not all limited. Look for example at this Wilmont, the guy that got after the crucifixion of Christ in the picture that Scorsese made. He has enough power to exercise a sort of a boycott. A lot of people were injured, I remember, out at the parking lot in Universal City. So their rights have to be considered, but again, no one is forcing these people to look at one of these cassettes. No one forces them at gunpoint to buy one and says, "You must look at that." Why should they care? I think maybe it's a feeling of being inadequate. The very fact that they're seeing a lot of wonderful sexual gymnastics occurring makes you wonder how exactly they conceived their children. Was it an immaculate thing? Did they grit their teeth? Were they afraid to make noise. Their fear makes you wonder about one of the most pleasureful activities in the world. How did these people who so condemn these types of activities, how did they conceive children?

*Well, they didn't do it on celluloid.*

Yeah, but even so, the whole business of having a great sexual encounter, so far as I'm concerned, is a lot of noise, a lot of gestures, a lot of activity, a lot of experimentation and so forth. That would be a good thing for Mike Wallace to interview some of these people and ask them some terribly embarrassing and intimate questions about their own tastes in copulation and things of that nature. Food for thought.

*How about the new rating, NC-17? Do you think it'll work? Is it a disguise for an X?*

With any of that stuff, I think once the public accepts it, it's okay. At first I thought NC-17 was kind of a lettering for the wingtip of an old Jenny. I think NC was one of the first sets of letters that indicated that you were a private flier. But I'm proud to say that my films got the first NC-17. *Beyond the Valley of the Dolls*, it was before *Henry and June*. That's what *Variety* said. I was very pleased. It'll give me an altogether different image now because there was always that tendency — X was like a skull and crossbones; it was evil. When I had the X it was worthwhile. But as soon as hardcore came into it, they got to XXX, so everything got the same kind of stigma. But now with the NC-17 the public is gonna accept it. It's one of those things. First, it's copyrighted. The X was never copyrighted. Anybody could attach an X. I think I got the second X, and that was on *Vixen*. The first X was a picture produced by Warner Bros. called *Girl on a Motorcycle*. It starred Marianne Faithfull. And from what I understand, Warner Bros. was so beside themselves they just put the damned picture on the film. They didn't even release it. But I did it with *Vixen*, and it was just great.

With *Vixen*, I think about 30 minutes of its 69 minutes length generally has to do with people having sex. It's an overabundance of sexual material, and the only way the ratings board could kind of deal with it was to make it less. They said, "If you cut out 11 minutes from *Vixen*, we'll give it an R." In spite of what anyone says, they're censors. It's an economic censorship. I tried it after I played it as an X for years . . . We put it out as an R and it died. The audience smelled it and realized it had been cut. And a picture called *Supervixens* — that is 21 minutes, I think excised, to get an R. I'm applying for an NC-17 now; there would be no cuts.

*And how successful do you think you'll be?*

Oh, no problem! They'll give them to me. It's a matter of me submitting my material, and they take the films and for some reason look at them. There's been some talk that even the hardcore people may be submitting some of their films for an NC-17. They're afraid now to come

up with any kind of guideline. They've asked for my films to make sure they're 71 minutes long or 94 minutes. Now what are they looking for? Maybe I'm slipping something in there . . . Then what category do they have? The X is no longer a category, is it? There's no longer an X, to my knowledge. That's puzzling.

**It's an economic—**

Well, the reason it happened was not from the goodness of Mr. Valenti's heart, by any means, because he was stoic about this whole thing, trying to hold it off. Because one of their greatest contributors, money-wise, was Universal Pictures. And they had a film that was worth several million dollars, and to give it an X [makes a backhanded slapping motion] was like, "Forget it." He wouldn't make a buck on that thing. Otherwise, if an independent appealed . . . There were a number of sexually-oriented independent pictures, all by and large rejected. They were given an X, or people would release them with no rating whatsoever.

Now you come out with some respectability. No children under the age of 17. So to answer your question, frankly it was a convenience to the majors. And I'm going to benefit from it. [Laughs.] I've heretofore used X on my cassette boxes, and there was a store that wouldn't carry X because of this idea that X is hardcore with the penetration and all that stuff . . . But now I may get into Blockbuster with my films because of the NC-17. If they take one NC-17, why can't they take another NC-17?

Some of the do-gooders have tried to say this is just another way of saying, "This is an X." Now the two selectmen in Massachusetts — they always elect those selectmen who look like Percy Kilbride — they overstepped their bounds. I think that's been quietly put to bed. One of the reasons is because it's a copyrighted rating. It's no longer an X.

**So that X has never hurt you because of its novelty, I think, at the time Vixen! was rated.**

Oh, yeah. X was certainly a benefit. We played . . . *Vixen!* made my life secure for the rest of my life. It was so successful, and largely because of Erica Gavin, who played Vixen. She had a quality about her that appealed to women just as much as men. I know for my third wife, it was mandatory viewing once a week. And when she viewed it, I benefited from it hugely there in the evening.

# Ted V. Mikels
## by Andrew Leavold

When I was a kid I used to stare in awe at the video covers for *The Corpse Grinders* and *Blood Orgy of the She-Devils*. Even at that age I could tell that these were not simple cheapjack nickel-and-dime horror shows; that they belonged to a strange filmic universe where the most bizarre imaginings were possible. I would remember the name Ted V. Mikels. I would watch his films in a kind of giddy delirium all through high school and beyond. They were certainly not normal, the films I later came to know as "exploitation" — more like moments of joyous madness from the universe of Ted V. Mikels.

A poster contact in Sydney, Ari Richards, announced out of the blue that he was heading to work on Mr. Mikels' latest film, a sequel to his 1969 cult favourite *Astro-Zombies* called (appropriately enough) *Mark of the Astro-Zombies*. My god, I thought, he's making a new movie! Little did I know that Ted never stopped working, and while film distribution may have changed since he ruled the drive-ins in the sixties and seventies with films like *The Doll Squad* and *The Worm Eaters* (!!!), his enormous output was sitting there waiting for the uncharted world of DVD to claim him.

Thanks to Ari I e-mailed Mr. Mikels and asked if I could interview him. From the moment I received his reply I understood why he is one of the best-loved characters in the trash universe; his warm, generous spirit makes and keeps friends instantly. He is also a walking encyclopedia of filmmaking from over 50 years in the business of doing it all — directing, producing, editing, distributing, right down to camera, stunts, lighting, dubbing (he was even the sound operator on the 1965 Ed Wood-scripted nudie, *Orgy of the Dead*!) Ted's films all have an unmistakable feel; along with Russ Meyer and John Waters he is your living, breathing all-American auteur. Plus his films are entertaining as hell! Unlike most filmmakers working in the exploitation field, Ted really knows how to deliver the goods. And I know he hates his films being labeled "trash," but I mean this in the most affectionate way — Ted V. Mikels is one of the all-time Trash Kings.

**Do you get people ringing you up and saying please let me work for you, let me be your apprentice?**

Oh yes, all the time. Had another one this afternoon. And who knows, we'll talk further. Of course, there are a lot of people out there that want to make films but they really don't have a way to get started.

**I guess everything is getting shot these days on Super-16 and High-Definition Video. It must be changing the actual way that films are being lit and being shot and things like that.**

The sad part about it is if people who are shooting video only rely on the monitor for their lighting, or rely on the iris and the camera itself for illumination, they bypass the art of lighting. And it looks like it. It's either crackling, sparkling, filled with jillions of little glitterspots, which destroy the look, or it's not lit properly at all so you have no definition. If they would learn motion picture lighting first, and then light for video, whether it's digital or non-digital, they would have a vastly superior quality. But they don't want to take the time to learn lighting. They figure the camera does it all, turn on the camera and take pictures!

*I've just seen so many films recently that usually go direct to video, of course, and they look so lousy. It's like there's a whole generation of filmmakers that kind of started in the mid-eighties onwards that have just forgotten how to actually make movies.*

Well, many of them have never learned it. It wasn't that they forgot, they

*A photograph of the prolific auteur, Ted V. Mikels*

haven't learned. A lot of people haven't learned yet that it takes something interesting to hold people's interest. They just can't shoot for their own satisfaction and think that everyone is going to like it. You've got to shoot for other people.

*I guess they all consider themselves 'artists,' and they must be beyond their audience!*

Well, if they can afford to play and spend the money to do it for their own ego satisfaction then more power to them. But unfortunately, most of these people are going to sit on their film and show it to friends after the barbecue, in the living room.

*Yeah, it sounds like a really expensive home movie. You've got a fully-functioning studio these days?*

I do. I opened it nine years ago. For 27 years I was in Hollywood, officed at the studios, the major studios — Columbia Pictures Studios, Samuel Goldwyn Studios, Allied Artists — my last office in Hollywood was in Universal Studios. I didn't care for Universal though — it was so big and so impersonal. I tell the story a lot of times that at Samuel Goldwyn Studios the guards would meet you at the gate and they would come out to the window of your auto and say, "How are you," "Good morning, sir," and all this sort of thing. Then they'd open the gate and you'd go in and feel like a king. But at Universal they'd give you a credit card pass so to speak, and you'd drive around to the backside of the lot, you'd stick your card in a box and the gate opens and you don't see a soul. It was not fun. I liked the more personal greeting . . .

At Columbia Pictures Studios it was the same way; they would meet you, talk to you for a bit, see how you are and how you're feeling. But in any event, my studio here is nothing like that. Mine is 2,500 square feet. However, with a balcony covering about a third of it, it's so crammed with filmmaking stuff—all sizes of lights, grip equipment, cables, cameras, post-editing bays. But I can still move it around and build a set here and a set there. For each movie I think I average about three sets in the little studio, just clearing walls, clearing space, putting up walls, bringing in furniture, whatever's required. But it's very serviceable, and you know you really need a headquarters when you're making a film. You either have to work out of a studio, or work out of a place where you store all the equipment. At the end of a shoot everybody goes back to the edit bay to look at what you've shot, see what it looks like, what it sounds like. I love that.

*So you're shooting on video these days?*

Well, I'm partial to it now. I use lighting techniques that I learned and taught hundreds of other people over the years, and using those same techniques makes my footage look like film — it even looks like 35mm. In fact, in some cases I think it looks better! Makes me feel better anyway, because it doesn't cost a buck and a half per second! A dollar and a half a second is what I figure that 35mm costs. And I've got four 35mm cameras — a great big Mitchell BNCR — magnificent piece of equipment. They're a quarter of a million dollars. Of course, they haven't made them like that for the last 18 years or so. Then I've got three Arriflexes. But even with all that, I thought I would never say I now prefer video because I was also a DP with the two major unions in this country, IATSE in Hollywood and NABET. I was on the committee that would give questions to new people wanting to get their DP acceptance. And I'd put them through the quizzes, along with a couple of other guys, both of whom got their Academy Awards.

I thought I'd never ever say that I prefer video over film. I thought I would never see the day that I would say that, and here I'm saying it! I've got digital cameras; I've got my Beta-SP . . . And the nicest part about it is that you have the combination of double system, and in a sense, it's like single system. Because if you're miking everything properly, you're functioning like it's a double system. Like the digital cameras have sixteen-bit sound which is CD-DAT quality, and that even supersedes some of the old equipment that we used to record on. Now, the Nagra is fine. I have a Nagra 4.2. I love it, used it for a *lot* of movies. But then you have to transfer it from the quarter-inch to 35-stripe to match the picture, sync it up in the sync-blocks, join your visual image of the slate clapping with the audio click, and then move on to the next step. It's a different world, there is a fascination to it, and editing on actual film will soon be a lost art.

***So it sounds like your movies are taking about a third of the time to put together and edit.***

Post-production averages three to four months. And that's on video *or* on film. And, in fact, I think I can work even faster on film, because I used to do a complete breakdown; in other words, you log all of your film and when you sync it and join it, you run it through the coding machines. Then you get ready to break it down, and that whole period takes about two weeks. But from that period, give me two to three weeks and I'd have a rough cut of the whole movie. Then, after the rough cut, you start fine-tuning it, figuring where you're going to put in your effects. Then you bring in your composer and let him get some idea of what kinds of music you're going to have to have. Then you start doing the audio effects. I always allowed 12 weeks for post-production. Twelve weeks from when I could break down the joined coded picture image and audio track. So now on video it takes about the same. I think that if you average two and a half, three minutes for an edit session, that's pretty good. And that's about what you do when you edit film, although sometimes I guess I could work faster with film because I was so used to it. Using the old Moviolas, you know, zing, zing, zing, zing, stuff goes through. If you want to make a change, you peel off the tape, insert or take out, and you're back in business. Not so with video! If you 're doing nonlinear video that's a different ballgame. And even though I bought a beautiful nonlinear system, I just can't get used to it. So I'm using some of the tricks that I used in making 'film' movies, and I've carried them over into my 'video' procedures, and so I've got a kind of a mixture.

***So you'd almost be able to teach a course in how to make 'film' on video?***

Something that is hard to teach is creativity. You can teach people the technical things, how to cut, when to cut, why to cut, what to cut to, and what to cut from. But if they don't have that creative touch, it may not work. They like to think that because they took a long time making a shot they ought to use it in the edit. It doesn't work that way.

***I always hear people argue that a director should never cut their own film, because they're always in love with their own shots.***

For beginning directors, that's true. But after you've done it for 30 years, you get very hard and you say, nope, it just doesn't play. It's too long, it's what have you. One of the toughest things I've had to deal with personally is the continuity of the images. Where, for example, you show somebody walking to the door on the interior, then outside you get them coming out of the door, walking to their car, and backing out of the parking place and driving off. Now, the modern way of doing that is you show someone putting their hand on the doorknob, the next thing their hand is on the steering wheel driving down the highway. There's a lot of that.

*Yeah, the jump cut.*

That was the toughest thing for me, to discipline myself to do. To move on with those cuts, get the show underway. And no matter how ruthless you are, you can go back. I can go back to anything I've done, and I can cut it. I can cut the heck out of it. I've had a lot of people tell me, why don't I go back and recut some of my oldies, you know? I don't want to. I like them the way they are. That was what was representative of what I was able to do then, and maybe I could make it better now, but I don't want to change anything. I'd rather make a new movie!

**Well, you wouldn't ask Michelangelo to go back and cut the nose off David, would you?**

So I won't go back and recut and rename my films. A distributor friend called me about three days ago to tell me he has some prints of *Doll Squad*. Well, when he released it in his territory in Texas he wanted to call it *Seduce And Destroy*! So I said okay. So he got another 10 or 12 prints from me, and he changed the title to *Seduce And Destroy*. I'm not sure that anyone would know that was *The Doll Squad*, except that it has Francine York, Michael Ansara, and all those people!

**And looks suspiciously like Charlie's Angels, but that's another story!**

And also, every once in a while somebody sends me a film — *Renegade Girls* or something like that — and they would send it to me saying, "This looks strangely like one of your films." So I would open it up, and the only thing different about it was the first second of the main title, and after that it's "Directed by Ted Mikels, written by . . .," the whole thing!

*Oh no . . .*

They had just ripped it off. That's the way the world goes. If you call them on it, they say, "Oh, we thought it was public domain."

**So what do you do, spend thousands and thousands trying to get back a couple of hundred?**

No, no, I don't. If I find somebody who's doing it illegally, I phone them up and I say, "Hey, I'm the writer, producer, director, I financed it, I edited it, I released it, I'm the copyright holder and the distributor. Now, tell me what rights you have!" [Laughs.] I've had to do that a few times.

**So do you retain the rights to most of your films?**

Well, the ones that I do on my own, yes. When I'm hired to make some for somebody else, I don't have those rights . . . Pictures like *The Black Klansman*. I have a piece of that, never saw anything of course. *War Cat*, also known as *Angel Of Vengence*, I spent 19 months making that! And that was the only film I didn't decide to edit right away, because Jeff Hogue and his partner were trying to take it back to Oklahoma, to have it edited by their friends back there. It turned out, they shipped it back and forth, and it went through airline X-rays a number of times. I finally agreed to do it, and when I got it the tracks were magnetized. "Now get on the wagon honey" would sound like *"clziztz clitztz kitzhz kitz!"*

What I did, rather than recopy — in other words make a new print of every spoken word of the film, and then have to code it, match it together with the track in sync — I went ahead and edited the picture with the garbled sound. Because I knew what it was, because I directed it, right? I made up a lot of the dialogue on the spot, because we had some sort of a script to begin with. When I took on the picture to direct it, I just gave everybody lines to speak. So I knew basically every word that was spoken. Then, after I cut it, I had to go back and transfer only the portions where I used the actual take. Then I had to take a big thick magnifying glass and put it over the ground glass viewer on the Moviola and then on top of that I used double magnifiers so I could take a pair of lips and put a word to it like "Get — on — your — horse."

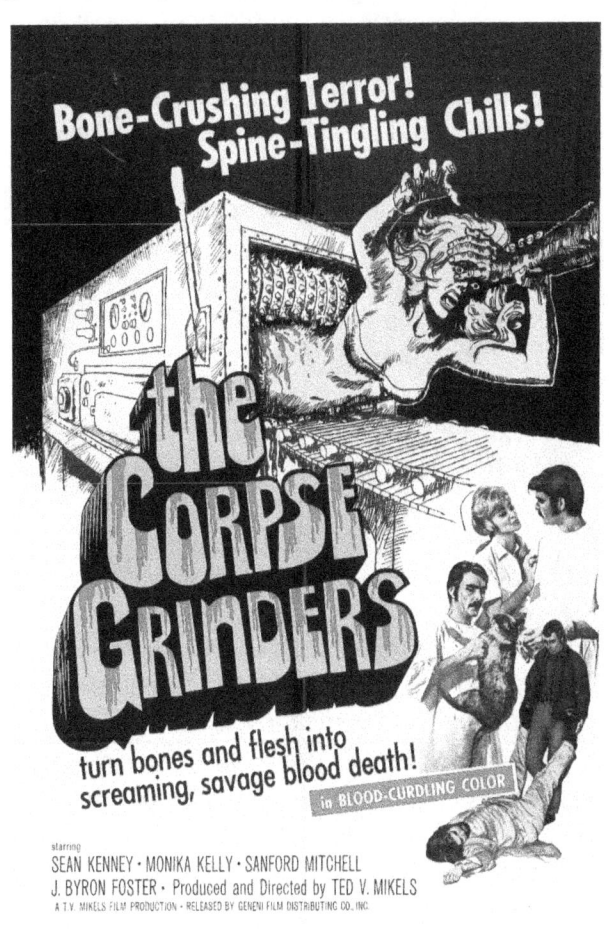

I'd have to watch the movements of the lips with the magnifying glass, and listen to the sound so I could synch it up. That was, I think, the toughest job of any editing I've ever done. In the entire film I had to replace every word. In a studio, that's what they call 'automatic dialogue replacement.' They run a loop, and the person would say, "Now get on your horse and get out of here," and they'd play it for him or her, the actors, they'd play it two or three times, and the next time they'd record it. The person would say, "Now get on your horse and get out of here," and the director would say, "Well, you need to be a little bit faster than that." "Now get on your horse and get out of here!" And you'd do it four or five times. But at least it's in sync with what they're looking at. But that's not what I had to do. *That* was tough. Anyway, that's what takes time on a lot of movies. So that editing period was obviously more than 90 days!

*So you said you had a piece of The Black Klansman and never —*

At one time, I had a piece of half the movies in Hollywood! But it doesn't mean anything, I'll tell you there. Everybody thinks that having a piece of a movie is great. I don't offer pieces of movies anymore. I did, too, at a time, even to investors. You get a percentage of whatever, when everything is recovered. But you know, it's too difficult. The world of film has changed so much, I don't look for investors; I look for people who want to have fun. I tell them, you might lose every dime. They don't want to hear that. So they don't invest.

*And if you make money, sometimes that's a beautiful accident.*

Yeah, it is. That's what happened on the original *Corpse Grinders*. It happened on a few other films, too. But it is an accident when it happens. You've got to remember, still there are many times more films that never recover their costs than do.

*Maybe 10 years later, yeah.*

I was explaining to someone just yesterday or the day before, if a film costs a hundred million to make, and it does 125 million at the box office, they'll be in debt for a long time. Because that 125 million at the box office is chipped away by advertising, television commercials, newspaper ads, radio, all sorts of promotions, then the theatres get their cut, distributor takes their cut . . . By the time it's applied against the cost of the movie, maybe only 15 or 20 of that $125 million goes to recover the cost! So when I was in distribution, meaning of mine and other people's pictures, I figured about seven percent came back to the producer. Seven percent of box office gross.

*That's incredible. When you think that most movies today cost about $70 to $100 million, your big studio films . . .and they just hope that one out of those 10 is a blockbuster!*

It takes quite a number of times the actual cost, in return at the box office, to make any money. The *LA Times* newspaper ran an article because on *Midnight Express* the people that made it had gotten Academy Awards and everything, and three years later, they still hadn't seen a dime! So Columbia Pictures got taken to task so to speak, and within two weeks the producers got a cheque for two hundred and thirty thousand. And the picture had grossed two hundred and thirty *million*, something like that. But they got $232,000; I think that's somewhere near the figure they got. But just "sloppy bookkeeping," they just didn't get around to giving any money back to the producers! So that's happened to me a *lot*. I'm about to help a friend who's writing a book on filmmaking. He's asked a lot of questions and if I answer them the way I'd *like* to, these people that read this book aren't going to want to make movies! [Laughs.] If they think they're going to make a lot of money, they're just dreaming.

**You've got the rights to your films. Do you see DVD as being kind of like a new frontier, or do you think it's just —**

Well, I think it is *the* new frontier. About 25 years ago, I jokingly used to talk about having holograms on the middle of my dining room table, where I could see a movie of mine in full dimension. I've talked about that off and on, and I think we'll see that day. I think a hologram on the middle of your dining room table giving you the full total multidimensional visual and audio of a movie one day will come. I don't know how they'd get around to putting cameras on a 360-degree circle without shooting the cameraman and all that, but maybe they could do a 180. And that still would be a pretty good hologram.

**Taking a slightly different track, which film of yours do you wish you hadn't made? Is there one black sheep in the flock that you wish would . . .**

After we made *Worm Eaters*, we showed it at 20th Century Fox. In the big screening room there — I always had champagne screenings at the studios after my movies — a good friend said, "Ted, let's take a little walk." So we walked around the lot there at 20th, and he said, "You know, Ted — is there any way you could get your name off of that movie?" [Laughs.] And people tell me that's their favourite one! The University of Washington rented it so many times, because it gave them more fun and more relief, people were going around and when someone did something stupid, they'd say "Worm him! Worm him!" They rented that film more than any other film. Of course, I never got a dime of that either. I don't know who they rented it from . . . but anyway, it was their favourite rental.

**Because that's on the Ted V. Mikels shelf in the (Trash Video) shop. That's on video in Australia, and that's a very, very popular renter.**

I'm trying to think, how did it get to Australia? There would be times I would make a deal, like I did a deal with somebody in London years ago, and I had made the deal for four of my films. I sent them all the prints and so on, and then they started selling rights all over Europe and who knows, the Far East and everywhere — but they didn't pay me! So I tried to cancel them, and they said, "Well, we didn't have a good print of *Girl In Gold Boots*," and I said I shipped them a total of about six prints, but the only excuse they could offer was they didn't have a good print of *Girl In Gold Boots*. So anyway, I canceled the contract, but too many countries had already bought rights from *them*. *They* never gave me any money; and that's the story of the film business.

*Amazing. Because I think they all came out on the same label (Star).*

Well, I know I never got anything out of it, so that's the way it goes. You just can't track 'em all down. There was a company — I don't know if it was Star or not — they put out some of my stuff. They made new jackets. They weren't like the jackets as you see on my website. My jackets on my website were all made from the one-sheets when I made the movie. It became the key art. But some of these people would made up new art, because they didn't have access to any legitimate source, so they'd make up their own.

*You see some shoddy stuff out there.*

I don't know Star at all, and I don't know who could have made a deal with them, and they may have paid somebody to be able to do whatever they do, but to my knowledge I never received a dime. The same thing in Korea. *All* my movies are in South Korea. Never sold one to South Korea, but they're all there. And again, I've never gotten a dime.

*The Black Klansman — that's the earliest of your films on video over here — and that was brought out by RCA Columbia.*

Really?

*Yeah. So if you never got to see any money from that, there are bloody crooks at Columbia!*

Well, see, I made my deal with Joe Solomon. And I was supposed to get fifteen percent of the profits. But even a year ago, when I talked to him, he's still alive, he said, well, they never did recover [laughs]. And you know, when I made the thing, I made it for $55,000. Did everything, you know, produce, directed it, edited it and all. And in the first week that it played in Newark it hit $25,000 gross. *One* theatre, *one* week — and I had made the movie for $55,000. It's hard to say why it turns out that people are able to say, gee, we didn't make any money on it, so you don't have any comeback. I could just go down the list — a lot of movies I've made.

*I'm sure it's heartbreaking if you actually sat down and make out a total of what you* should *have gotten.*

Yeah, well, look at *Astro-Zombies*. Never got a dime. Writing, producing, directing, shot half of it, editing, 13 months there of my life. Never got a dime. However, they say live and learn. Anymore, I don't like to have other involvements. So I can just do it on my own. And then any money that does come theoretically will come to me. If any comes. But I don't mean to paint such a bleak picture of the business. Obviously I haven't done anything else but make movies for the last almost 50 years, so evidently there's something that has treated me okay. Advances from here and there—we sold Japan five of my movies for home video for a nice advance;

like we sold France one or more pictures where they buy all rights, theatrical, television, home video, everything, for a given number of years. Usually not to exceed five years. And then some places you sell the rights over again after that time. So I can't really say it's been that bad to me.

# Bill Rebane
## by ED Tucker

**EDITOR'S NOTE:** *Writer/producer/director Bill Rebane is best known for low budget horror films such as* Invasion from Inner Earth *and* The Giant Spider Invasion. *Herschell Gordon Lewis crafted the film* Monster-a-Go-Go *out of the footage from Rebane's abandoned film* Terror at Half Day. *In addition to these accomplishments, Rebane also ran unsuccessfully for governor of Wisconsin in 1979 and introduced the world's first 360-degree motion picture process, which has since led to the Cinemax process and the Rotascope camera.*

**The first film I see you having a credit on is Twist Craze from 1961. Is that correct?**

I was the writer, the creator, the producer and actually directed the director on that one. A fellow by the name of Alan David, who put up a very small piece of change for that picture at the last minute, was a wannabe director. He had not succeeded with anything theatrically in Chicago, so I basically gave him a director's credit.

**Was Twist Craze a national release?**

Yes. That was a phenomenal success for me. As soon as the film was done, it was only a 10-minute one-reeler. It opened at the Oriental Theater in Chicago, and the owner matched it up with *Pocketful of Miracle s*— Frank Capra's picture. It ran for an extended time with three or four holdovers, and it made three times the budget back just at the Oriental Theater in Chicago. On the basis of that, it went to the Paramount Theater in New York and when it opened there, I got a phone call from none other than Sam Arkoff at American International Pictures. I was floored. He said to me, "Hey, kid, I hear you got a winner going." I said, "Well, I like to think so." And then he said, "How would you like to come out to LA because we're interested in the picture?"

I made an appointment to see him, and I flew out there. I got the red carpet treatment; his lawyers picked me up at the airport with a limousine. I got wined and dined and within 24 hours I had signed a contract for $10,000 cash for *Twist Craze*. AIP took it on internationally because they needed 10 minutes more for a picture they were releasing. I think it was called *Twist All Night*. They added it to that release. It was actually edited onto the beginning, and it played in thousands of theaters all over the world.

**Was there any possibility of a continued relationship with American International after that?**

Yes, that actually set off *Terror at Half Day/Monster-a-Go-Go*. Twist Craze kicked everything off. I made a phenomenal amount of money for a short subject. All of the investors tripled their money. They were happy as larks. I went into production on another 20-minute short called *Dance Craze*, which also played the Oriental Theater. It included all kinds of other dances because, at that time, there were things happening in the music industry, like the La Bostella and the Go Go. I made *Dance Craze* a two-reeler, which was a much richer film, and that was bought, ultimately, by Crown International Pictures.

About this same time, Sam Arkoff asked me what I was going to do next. Now at that time, American International was like a mini-major company, and Arkoff had this huge desk in his office. Here I was, sitting in front of this desk and

*A photograph of director Bill Rebane at his studio circa 1978.*

*feeling like a dwarf, and I told him I was working on something on the science fiction level. He told me that wasn't a bad idea, but that he needed a picture that had something to do with car racing because Roger Corman was involved with AIP at that time and was doing those kinds of pictures. He asked me if I would do a picture on the Indianapolis 500, for instance, and I said, "Sure I would." I was headstrong at the time, though, and I really had my mind set on doing Terror at Half Day.*

**Where did the idea for Terror at Half Day come from?**

I had bought my first house in Wheeling, Illinois, and I had to commute through Half Day, back and forth to Chicago. Half Day was a little villa just past Wheeling, and the name intrigued me so much. I was thinking, what the hell can I do for an interesting picture, and Half Day had to fit in there somehow. I was set to do a science fiction picture, but a monster never really figured into this. As I developed my first screenplay — something I had never attempted to do before — I wanted to do something more on the lines of a Hitchcock sci-fi picture. Exploitation was not in my vocabulary at that time, unless it came to something timely like *Twist Craze* or in the musical era.

It took months for me to get everything straight for *Half Day*. I had a friend who was a beautician that wanted, in the worst way, to be an actor. His name was George Perry. He played the part of one of the scientists. I knew then that George had a tremendous ego but he was a possible investor. As you know, in this business one of the worst things that can happen to you is getting an investor who also wants to be in the picture. Well, it happened, but I figured I could make him into an actor. As you can probably tell by the picture, he didn't quite make it! He tried hard, but he was still stagey and stiff.

**Didn't you have some screen time in that film in one scene?**

Yes. It was the scene where the monster attacks the couple in the car. It was done out of both necessity and ego. At that time, I wanted to be a dancer, singer, and actor more than I wanted to be a director. I will let you in on a little secret — frankly, I didn't know enough about producing and directing at that time or the technical aspect of production. That's the reason I surrounded myself with union people. Frank Phifer was a friend of mine who was a cameraman from Chicago — probably one of the best. The first editor I had came from Jack Lee Productions in Chicago, also an experienced theatrical editor. I tried to surround myself with people who knew what they were doing.

Some of the equipment we used I was talked into because it was cheap. It was very thrilling at the time to have a big camera that really looked like a big production, so we used an MC Mitchell. With a blimp it required a real dolly to operate it. You try to put a 2,000-pound camera on a tripod and you need a big crew. So I got a Houston Fearless dolly. There was no production manager on this shoot; I was it. I realized I would need a big truck to move this equipment around. I had friends in Chicago everywhere that had van lines, so I got a semi for free with a hydraulic platform. It could carry this huge Houston Fearless dolly and this MC Mitchell camera, which weighed something unbelievable, and then we had to go out in the middle of a field to shoot. If I had known then what I knew 20 years later, it would have been absurd to even entertain that kind of operation.

**Did you start Terror at Half Day with a completed script?**

Yes, I did. That was one thing I knew from my early days in Germany — you have to have a script.

**How far into the production did you get before you hit financial difficulties?**

I had two initial backers on that, including George Perry. I think we did about three weeks of shooting before we started running short on money. Then Helen Kline entered. She was a friend I met at a supper club who happened to own the gift shops at the Hilton hotels. She thought I was a very up-and-coming young kid, very talented. She offered to put money into it. I managed to keep Peter Thompson in the loop, and June Travis had been signed; she was a local from Chicago. June Travis' husband, Fred Freelow, also came through with some money. This was the first time I was introduced to deal-making where you "pay" the actor and they kick the money back towards production.

**How far along were you with the film before things ground to a halt?**

I would say about three-fourths. That's why I can never understand how it turned out the way it did. We had a pretty much completed picture before Herschell [Gordon Lewis] took it over.

**You were missing the ending, weren't you?**

That, I think, was one of the problems.

**Now I have to ask you a question that's been plaguing me for years. How was Terror at Half Day supposed to end? As it stands now, the monster is being chased through the sewers and then it just disappears. They find the space suit floating in the water and that's it.**

To be honest with you, ED, I just can't remember how it was supposed to turn out. Knowing myself, and knowing where I wanted to go in life with movies, I would have to guess that it was going to be a happy and good ending. I don't even think I have a copy of the script. I have every screenplay and dialogue transcript of everything I ever did except that.

*I hate to think the original ending is lost to history.*

I'm trying to think back. It had to be a reasonably logical and classy kind of an ending. The worst part is that I've seen *Monster-a-Go-Go* maybe twice in the last 40 years, and maybe that's why I have so much trouble remembering.

**Do you have any idea what you would have needed to complete the film?**

I think we would have needed around $20-$25,000 to complete it at that time. I had Peter Thompson scheduled for about two weeks. When it started running out of money, the biggest problem we had was that we were losing our star. He was committed to another project so we only had him for two weeks and the two weeks was up. Because of the loss of Peter Thompson, I thought at that point we had lost the picture totally.

I took the rushes and I screened them for Allied Theaters, which was a big, strong, wealthy chain of theaters at that time. I believe I still have a letter from Allied Theaters commending me on my efforts and stating that it looked like I had a very playable science fiction picture and that they would book it. With that letter, I went back to LA and got back with Sam Arkoff. He looked at the rushes and said he wanted to see the finished product. Because of their busy schedule of releases, they were not prepared on the spur of the moment to make a major commitment like I was asking for. At that time, I had a friend named Dok Stanford who was a combination screenwriter, music writer, and had been in the business for a long time. When I met him, we became good friends and he had introduced me to a lot of people in Hollywood. Long story short, Dok said he would come to Chicago and help arrange for some money to finish the thing and, if need be, rewrite the script in such a way that we would not need Peter Thompson. So he rewrote the script with me and wrote himself in as Peter's brother. All of a sudden, the film had a new star and Dok Stanford was it. With him taking over the lead part, we shot a second session which brought the film closer to being completed but didn't quite make it.

Herschell entered the picture at this point because I didn't have a union crew anymore, and he was the only game in town that would tackle anything as a non-union cameraman and production manager. He was a one-man show like I was basically, but Herschell had experience. I was just a kid starting out. Herschell had a company at that time called BI&L Distributing, and it was through that company that I made the deal for *Monster-a-Go-Go*, but I had no idea at the time what the title was going to be. I pretty much counted on it being *Terror at Half Day*, the way it was originally named.

**Where were you in the production of the film when you made this deal with Herschell Gordon Lewis for him to take over the picture? It's amazing that he would take what was there — without the ending — and still release it.**

It was after all the shooting when it was three three-quarters completed or better. This was six to eight months later. As I recall, he shot the scene in the park where the girls are laying in the grass. I'm sure he made a deal with Henry Hite for that scene, to come out of the bushes and scare the girls. Herschell invited me up to his office on several occasions to watch some of the edited footage on his Movieola, but I never participated in that. I didn't have anything else to do with the film from that point forward.

**It seems like there was a considerable gap between Terror at Half Day and your next feature, Invasion from Inner Earth, in 1974.**

Well, let me see if I can piece a couple of things together here . . . I think I used part of the money I got from Herschell for *Terror at Half Day* and went back to Europe. I took a position with a studio there, and I took it very seriously. It was at a time in 1963 or 1964 that was commonly known as runaway production time. The prices in Europe for productions were cheap, and American producers were looking for studio sources to participate in production and basically shoot at a cheaper rate. So I went to Germany and became the representative for the studio in the U.S. for all co-productions.

I worked in Germany until 1966 when I took a road trip to Wisconsin to find some property to build a studio on. I had three children at that time and I figured Chicago wasn't the place for me to raise my kids. I had occasionally worked for a friend of mine in Chicago as various things like a production manager, assistant director, and assistant cameraman—everything assistant. He kept calling me and giving me jobs until I was inundated with work. Now remember, I wasn't an editor or technical person at that time in the '60s. It was a self-learning process as I kept getting that stuff dumped on me. I was doing commercials, industrial films, and corporate image stuff.

By the time we moved to Wisconsin, I was never home. I was traveling to Indianapolis, to St. Louis, to everyplace in the country, shooting industrial films. I was able to go out and shoot what I needed to on location and then bring it home to work on. I would come home and do the editing, deliver the product and get paid. I was able to start building my little production studio in Wisconsin.

**Had the desire to create a finished feature been hanging around with you ever since Terror at Half Day?**

It had. I think under it all I knew I was going to return to theatrical production, but I had no idea it was going to be sci-fi/horror stuff again. I realized by that time what the words exploitation and timeliness meant. I realized it would be too cost and effort intensive to try and raise $2 or $3 million for something like a musical, so *Invasion from Inner Earth* took hold, because I knew the terrain I had and that there had to be a way to take advantage of it.

The next question was where to get the actors. I figured there had to be some around at the University. I contacted a longtime friend of mine, Jack Willoughby, who was a director of cinematography at some of the major studios in Hollywood. Jack offered to come to Wisconsin to work on the picture, and I got a crew together of about five or six people. So between Jack and I and a few helping hands we did *Invasion from Inner Earth*.

**Where did the script for that come from?**

I wrote that and my wife helped me.

**Was it specified in the script that the aliens were going to be represented solely by red lights and smoke bombs?**

Yes and no. I think that developed as the first draft was done. As a matter of fact, it became a joke on the set. "What's this film all about?" "It's about a red light!" But we kept using them because we had nothing else to use.

**Didn't you actually build a flying saucer that is seen briefly in the film?**

That was a trick. How to get a flying saucer made? I sat for hours on end constructing little model saucers and they were all duds. I finally got one that looked real if you looked at it from a distance. I took fish wire and tied it to the saucer. Then I went to the highest point on the house and I hung it over the side and moved it back and forth. You just caught glimpses of it, I think. It was a whole lot of fun.

**Was the ending of the picture the way it was originally planned in the script?**

That was an afterthought. Originally the film ended with the last two people on the railroad tracks. Then I extended it to the children in the field, Adam and Eve, so to say.

***I actually saw that film at a kiddie matinee around 1977 when I would have been 10 or 11 years old. You can't imagine the howls and screams that came from a theater full of pre-teen kids when those two semi-naked toddlers appeared on the screen. That was the audience I saw it with.***

Yes, I can. That sounds amazing.

***I thought they were going to start tearing the seats out of the theater. I think it played well to that audience, though. There were a lot of comedy bits that went over well with that age group. All these years later I can still remember all of this, so it was a memorable picture.***

[Laughs.] I didn't know anybody would think of it that way!

**So *Invasion from Inner Earth* was finished. Did it have a regular theatrical run outside of kiddie matinees?**

Yes, it did. The original title, by the way, was not *Invasion from Inner Earth*. It was *The Selected*. That was the true title and the title we released it under. I sold it to Sun International and they retitled it *Invasion from Inner Earth*.

**So you went from your first completed feature, which was low budget with a no-name cast to Giant Spider Invasion, which had a considerably larger budget and, by B movie standards at least, an all-star cast.**

After *Invasion from Inner Earth* I did a series of six bank training films on theft. They were crime training films. I also did about five educational films. Steve Brodie was in one of those. Steve and I had become very close friends. He loved coming to Wisconsin. He was considered a has-been, but he had a very recognizable face. Steve and I sat in a ton of Hollywood bars trying to think of how we could get people for this film. That's how we got Alan Hale. Once Alan Hale was in, everyone else just came on automatically — Leslie Parrish, Barbara Hale, and Bill Williams. Robert Easton came in through Tain Bodkin, the actor who played the preacher. Tain Bodkin was a student of Robert Easton in one of his voice classes and suggested him because he wanted to do him a favor.

Tain introduced us to Bob Easton, and Bob took the first draft of the script and said, "You've got to be kidding, guys." The distributor, Brandon Chase, said the same thing. The first script was atrocious. It was written by Richard Huff, a commercial writer in Madison, Wisconsin, who wanted to be a writer but didn't have a clue about what writing a screenplay was all about. We kicked a whole bunch of ideas around, and then I took a treatment to Brandon Chase. He liked it, but there were no giant spiders. The whole thing had to do with black holes and was more technically oriented. Then I massaged it to a point where it became doable as a low-budget picture.

We didn't know how much money we could raise at that time. Richard Huff put me in touch with William Dyke, who was the former mayor of Madison and a lawyer. He went out and started raising the money for the film and came up with the idea of it being a tax shelter; that's how it was financed. By the first day of shooting there was no money in the bank — not a penny. The investors actually showed up on the first day of shooting to decide if they wanted to put any money in it. Then it came in in dribbles like $50,000 at a time.

**So you started the film with no money? That couldn't have been easy.**

We were having coniptions. I was trying to do everything myself and everyone kept saying I needed help, so I hired a line producer out of Canada, Tony Cromrieter. All of a sudden I found myself with four producers — Bill Dyke, Richard Huff, Tim Gillet, an investor, and this guy from Canada, Tony Cromrieter, who was also going to be the line producer. We didn't even have a finished script at this point. I don't know how

Brandon Chase got talked into this one! The only thing we got from communications back and forth with him was, "Make the spiders big — as big as you can . . . I want giant spiders!"

We kept drafting and submitting new stuff until Brandon Chase said, "You need a new writer." Bob Easton was a writer, so he said, "Why don't you give me a shot at this?" Bob Easton, who was a highly professional individual, got into the writing, and he had to put up with Richard Huff who didn't have an ounce of an idea about what it was all about. These two started fighting about story concept and characters. Bob Easton came to Wisconsin a week or two before the shoot started and locked in a lakeside cabin to write so many pages a day of the script. This German producer from Canada would threaten him — if he didn't write so many pages a day, he wouldn't get fed! Bob Easton was sitting in his cabin pounding out pages that would get filtered to Richard Huff in Madison, who seldom came up. Then it would go back to Bob Easton. All the while, I'm on the set shooting and I have no idea where the ending is going. That's how it was shot — day by day. Basically, Bob Easton and I created the story as it went.

*So it's amazing that the film is as coherent as it is.*

It is indeed. The biggest problem the film had was my special effects man. He was a jack of all trades and I loved him dearly.

*Actually he was a Jack Daniels of all trades, wasn't he?*

Yeah, kind of. He was a fellow named Bob Millay from Chicago, but we should have called him Bud Weiser! Before noon he had a case of beer in his stomach! The spiders started out fantastic. I have all the still photos of how they evolved — the welding process. The welder that did this was a very creative old man. We needed a brainstorm for how to build this really big spider for Brandon Chase. We also realized there were pages in the daily script that called for the spider to be on top of a house and we thought, How in the hell are we going to do this? How are we going to get a Volkswagen and the whole nine yards up there? That's when we decided to build another one that was real light and could be lifted with a crane.

*You had a couple of other spiders in the film, as well, including the one in the web that attacks the car.*

Yes, that was our medium-sized spider. That one also had its weaknesses. If we filmed it straight on and tried to show any detail, it looked worse than it was. That's why you only see a few quick cuts of it in the film.

*I thought the spider that attacks Leslie Parrish was actually pretty effective.*

You mean the one that jumped on my wife! That was Leslie running into the building, but my wife, Barbara, getting jumped on. Leslie was not that great of a trooper, especially after she fell into a big cow pie. It was 110 degree weather and she was walking through the field with Robert Easton. She was supposed to trip and take a fall backwards. What nobody knew was that right there was a fresh cow pie. She was absolutely livid.

**Where did you get the real live spiders from?**

Oh, the tarantulas? Those came from a pet shop. Kevin Brodie, my assistant director, Steve's son, brought them from California. I think we had about six of them all living in my basement.

**That was all? It seemed like there were more of them in the film.**

It looked like it. We really only had two trained spiders. One of their names was Tanya, she had a bald ass. Bob Millay, the special effects guy, he took a liking to the tarantulas. One got killed when Barbara Hale knocked the briefcase off the car and he quit after that. It was a chaotic moment where she was supposed to brush the case off the car. She brushed too hard and it fell off the car and one of them got squished. It happened to be Tanya.

**So there was one fatality during the shoot. Did any of the actors have any problems working with the tarantulas?**

No. None whatsoever. Even Leslie Parrish, who was having an asthma attack during the scene where the spiders are on the bed, was okay with them. That was real panic on her face in that scene.

**Where did the idea for the spider that pops out of the drawer come from?**

That was impromptu. It was about a foot long and made the same day we shot the scene because I insisted we needed one in the drawer for shock value. That's where Bob Millay really shined. When it came to dreaming up quick things and doing them on the spot he could do that really well. The problem is that he was drinking too much beer. Today you have drug problems on film sets. Back then it was booze.

Steve Brodie almost bit the dust in that scene where the spider comes over the hill. Like I said, it was 110 degrees and he was soused up something terrible. He had to run and do a bit where he was falling and he almost had a heart attack! Then, in the last bit with the spider implosion, one of the young grips got too ambitious and wasn't listening. He got zapped during the explosion and ended up with third-degree burns on his shoulder and arm.

**Is it true that Giant Spider Invasion was one of the highest grossing films of 1975?**

Yes. Absolutely. Without question it was my most financially successful film. We brought that in for exactly $230,000. It was immediately successful and the big grosses came in in the first six months. It did well in the theaters, and then, I believe, it had five ABC network screenings. *Alpha Incident* also became a pretty fair financial success.

*Alpha Incident was your next film after Spiders?*

Yes, that was 1977. After *Spiders* we went right on and did a picture that I personally liked, *Alpha Incident* with Ralph Meeker. The original title was *Gift from a Red Planet*, but early on it was changed to *The Alpha Incident*. It was a tremendous challenge for me and I thought I pulled it off. Maybe that's why Paramount Pictures picked it up as a co-feature to *Star Wars* in the Western hemisphere. It was a slow picture, the old fashioned way. It was a drama and I found it to be a tremendous challenge.

When I wrote the script, I had to come up with something that would only involve a handful of people in the cast, and maybe in just one room. I expanded it a little bit into exteriors and two or three locations, but basically everything was shot on this little thirty-by-forty sound stage.

*It seems to me that you were going for a feature length version of an episode of The Twilight Zone.*

Yes, in a way. The expanding head effect was the first of its kind ever done on screen. *Scanners* went on to do something very similar. If there is any of my pictures that I don't mind seeing again or looking at or remembering, it's *Alpha Incident*. It's a decent picture and there are no creatures in it!

*After your success with Spiders, why did you step back to a smaller budget picture?*

*Alpha* was around $200,000. I went with a smaller picture because I wanted some dramatic recognition at that point and *Alpha* was tight and well written. My cousin, Ingrid Neumayer, wrote the script with me and did the final screenplay. With bigger names and a bigger budget it could have been a major picture. This was a totally different concept than *Spiders*. I think I was disgusted at how *Spiders* had been put together without a script. I wanted to do something that was fully scripted and well thought out, and *Alpha* gave me that opportunity.

*So now you had two successful pictures under your belt. Where did you go from there?*

I was always trying to take advantage of the locations surrounding the studio in Wisconsin. I never wrote a script without knowing what I could use for scenic and production values. I was sitting by the lake that was part of our property one day when I had, I guess you would say a brain fart, and came up with the idea for *Rana: The Legend of Shadow Lake*. I wanted to do something that was more of a sci-fi adventure type of picture with this one.

*Did you fund Rana yourself or were there outside investors?*

I personally, and the studio, invested in almost all of the pictures we did. On Rana, we had one other partial investor from Holland who was a fantastic guy, but otherwise it was all me. It was almost unheard of at that time for a producer to put his own money into a production. Rana went almost flawlessly. It was an absolute delight.

**Who designed the frog creature costume for Rana?**

That was originally designed by Tom Schwartz. The head was an original done from scrap drawings we made. Dale Kyphers came up with two versions of it. One was almost identical to the Creature from the Black Lagoon, so I nixed that. The other one was far from that so we went with it. I think Dale did the first rendition of a sculpture and then Tom Schwartz completed it all.

**Was Rana released in the US?**

Yes, we had US distribution for that. That was the beginnings of our going into distribution on our own. I made a deal with a stateside distributor in Denver. It was released in the Midwestern states. It was a regional theatrical release. I remember that because I made up 2,000 posters for that. Most of them were left at the studio when we lost it. *Rana* had tremendous foreign distribution. It did excellent in almost all foreign markets. It was also bought by the armed forces for broadcast.

**With Rana doing well in foreign distribution, what did you have in mind for your next picture?**

I was planning another big one and went into the biggest budget picture we made at that time, believe it or not, $400,000. The budget started out at $200,000, and it went $200,000 over budget. That was *The Capture of Bigfoot*.

**How did you decide on a Bigfoot movie?**

It was a hot topic, timeliness with good exploitation values. It was a well-planned picture, well scripted. I don't think there was anything wrong with the story except we didn't expect a winter with four feet of snow and 30-below weather for a six-week period. It was one of the worst winters Wisconsin had ever seen. We were shooting in 35mm and Panavision. These were the Panavision cameras, not Panaflex—the full-sized ones. We had to try to get those into the woods in four feet of snow, when we couldn't even get the snowmobiles out of the snow! The whole picture was basically shot in the studio backyard. We had 360-degree production because we could set the camera up in one spot and then turn it 90 degrees and it was a different scene.

I always had wonderful luck with the special effects guys. Dale Kyphers was the one on *Bigfoot* and he was fabulous. He was a fabulous prosthetics man, but he only had experience making museum pieces. Now you have to take into consideration that the Bigfoot costume had to be light and easy to move in for a person. He never dreamed of that. When I got the costume, I think it weighed close to 80 pounds. We had hired this huge wrestler and we had to put the costume on the floor and have the guy crawl in horizontally. That's how bad it was. Then we had to help him stand up, and he couldn't move!

**Were you able to use that costume or did you have to make another one?**

I had a visitor from Canada who came up to help with distribution. He was a tall young man about six-two or six-three. I said, "Guess what? You have to play Bigfoot!" We retailored the suit and took all of the padding out of it, cast his face in plaster to make a new prosthetic, and we had a new Bigfoot. The wrestler couldn't move in that heavy costume, and on top of that he had bad legs, so here we go with a new Bigfoot and then the weather started in. We put the prosthetic face piece on the inside where it was 67 degrees, and the moment he went outside in the 30-degree weather the sweat would make it slide right off his face. So we had to try to get the cameras into the woods under these conditions, get the actor going, and stay away from deteriorating prosthetics. It was a nightmare. This went on through practically the entire shoot. The investor was going bananas. He kept saying, "I have to sell more stuff to support this habit!"

Luckily, as we were close to finishing everything, I called Larry Woolner at Dimension Pictures. I remember this clearly. In the middle of February, this big Hollywood guy and his wife who wrote the checks visited Wisconsin. I had to bring him in from the road with a snowmobile to the screening room. He looked at the footage and said, "Let's make a deal because I think this picture has lots of legs." He offered us 30 percent of the gross, no deductions.

**So you jumped on that?**

Well, you have to remember that I had an investor partner and we were into his pocket for about $375,000 at this point. I told him about it and he said — I will never forget this — "Bill, if Larry Woolner is willing to offer 30 percent of gross, I bet you someone out there will offer us a better deal than that." I thought he was crazy. I told him if he wanted to turn it down, it was his call. I had given him the opportunity to be in the business side of things, so we told Larry Woolner we would have to think about it. Well, guess what? There was no better deal. So then the investor says we should think in terms of self-distribution. I told him it was going to cost more money to distribute a picture, so he flew to Denver and made a deal with the lab for 50 prints of the film, and this was $1,000 a print at that time. He put it on his credit card. I was stuck with 50 prints and a very short time to get the bookings. So I went into the distribution business. I called all my old friends that I knew, even back to the days of Herschell Gordon Lewis. I made a deal with a guy in Detroit to open it in 50 theaters in Michigan. We got the papers and signed the deal so that we would be in charge of our own destiny and then found out there were no advertising dollars.

*So you had everything ready to release a film and no way to tell anyone about it?*

My investor was tapped out, so the picture opened in 50 theaters with only the minimum ads provided by the theaters, and the grosses were tremendous! They were fantastic for a 50-theater book with no advertising; there were some full houses. We had blown the impact of an opening, so we couldn't move to anywhere else in the country with no distributing dollars. So I made a deal with Western Cine-Distributors in Denver who took the picture on, played it in the theaters in the Midwest for about six months and then went bankrupt.

Now I found myself not only in the distribution business, but in the foreign distribution business. The only way we could recover any money would be in foreign sales. That prompted me in 1981 to become a full foreign distributor. We went to the Milan market and Cannes Film Festival and started selling territories. I think we got about a third of our money back. That was a disaster.

The strange thing about this business of distribution is that I know people who made a film for $100,000 or $200,000, went through all the efforts, and the pictures never saw the light of day. I can say that every picture we produced was distributed on a worldwide basis and got maximum international exposure. If nothing else, I can make the claim that I have never had a picture end up on the shelf.

*Did things go better on your next film, Demons of Ludlow?*

That is another film that I don't mind seeing. Short of a weak actor, I think it is one of my favorite ones. Again, lots of production values—a $200,000 wonder. *Demons* was a special project. It was kind of a ghost story. One thing that made it a little stronger than a ghost story is a horror element. By that time, my distributors were telling me they liked the production values in my films, but they needed more blood and guts. I told them I would see what I could do. That's how *Demons of Ludlow* was born and then became a little stronger than the script actually called for.

*So you intentionally ramped up the gore?*

The goriest thing in there is a decapitation that is extremely realistic — almost too realistic. It had no names, no star value, but it was cohesive. It was shot in the winter time on a new 60-by-80 sound stage I had just finished. We built every set to order. I think we had eight sets for that. This was also the first film I was director of photography on as well as directing. I did the camerawork, I did the set design — I loved it. I worked with a small crew; I think we had four or five people on it.

*Did Demons play theatrically in the US?*

Yes, it did. It had a theatrical release, a video release, television and heavy foreign release. By that time, I was in full distribution of foreign sales, so the market was really good to us.

*Your next picture was a very low-budget production even by your previous standards.*

Yes. We needed an interim picture and we were at a loss for material. We needed something for the next Cannes Film Festival. I had a friend who owned a place in northern Wisconsin that I had complete access to, so we wrote a story around that since we were desperate for a little picture. That's how we ended up with *The Game*. We had a super low budget on that one — something like $75,000. I knew I could come up with a third of it. I flew to London and talked to a friend of mine in distribution, Alan Raynor, and he said he would love to do it. He put up $25,000. Then I went to Los Angeles and talked to Israel Shockit, my other distributor who handled foreign sales, and he came in, too. I think we all had $25,000 in it. We shot the picture in two weeks.

*The Game is quite a change from something like Demons of Ludlow. It's much more of a murder mystery type of film, which is completely different from anything else you had done.*

That's true. It made all of its money back. It was sold to a major Canadian distributor and did very well in the foreign territories.

*So your next film after that was* **Blood Harvest** *with Tiny Tim?*

Yes, that would have been the summer of 1985. A couple of young filmmakers from Minneapolis visited the studio with a script titled *I'll Be Waiting*. It was not workable; it was a bad script and I told them so. Two friends of mine and I did some brainstorming and rewrote the whole story. We actually didn't use any of the material they brought us. I went into a joint venture with them whereby they supplied a portion of the money, and I supplied the studio, the staff, the equipment, the post-production, and the distribution.

Then I realized the time had come and that another picture without name value wouldn't fly that well. Tiny Tim had just done a concert for me the year prior at the studio as a special promotion. We became close friends and I thought of him. He had never acted before, but he had a name and a following, so I took a stab at it.

*When you wrote the script, did you have him in mind for it?*

Oh yes, very definitely. I wanted to shoot this one and, for anyone, shooting and directing at the same time is not the easiest chore. You have a lot of things to think about — a lot of things on your mind. I decided to let Leszek Burzynski produce the picture and I would direct and shoot it. Again, it was a very small crew. I like working with six or eight people at best because it gives you a certain amount of control and no waste. Leszek Burzynski would always stand behind me and say, "Bill, more sex, more blood, more guts — remember that." *Blood Harvest* was really the first exploitation picture I made.

My partner in England who was in distribution with me said he might have a buyer for me. I flew to England with the rushes and I sold the picture to an English company for $250,000 cash, up front, before it was even finished. This was under the condition that they could bring their editor over from England to finish the editing at the studio. This is the idiosyncrasies of the British! Their editors are better than anyone else; they have to have their own editor for them to be able to do it. Leszek Burzynski was from England, too, so now I have a British producer and a British distributor. If you want nightmares, boy you get them from the British! Americans can't hold anything to them when it comes to directing, producing, editing, you name it. They were the boss!

I really didn't care because I had basically ended up financing this picture myself, and now I had a big chunk of cash. The $250,000 was only an advance on distribution; I didn't actually sell the picture. Then, I had to help them get a worldwide release because they were a new distribution company, so I teamed them up with New World Pictures, whose president at that time was Robert Reeling. They negotiated a $600,000 contract of which I would have received a portion.

*Was this before or after the British editor finished the film?*

This was after he finished the film and before I had the nervous breakdown. At the same time this was going on, the English distributor wanted to buy the studio and I didn't want to sell. I was being threatened with strong-arm tactics. I finally told them to do whatever it was they were going to do, and they opened up a studio in Eagle River, Wisconsin, about 60 miles from us. They made two $50,000 pictures and went bankrupt.

*Your next film was a real departure from your previous work — a humorous family picture.*

I was done with the blood and guts, and monster trucks were a big thing at that time. *Twister's Revenge* was a totally different ballgame. I had a lawyer friend in Chicago and he said he thought it was time I got out of the monster/horror/sci-fi stuff and moved on to something that was fun. He thought he was a writer, too, so we created *Twister's Revenge* with monster trucks.

We got two brand new Army tanks for nothing, demolished a lot of buildings, caused a lot of havoc in the neighboring areas there, and blew up a bunch of buildings — all for the nice sum of about $95,000. This was 1987 and we did the whole thing, lock, stock, and barrel, for $95,000. I took my investor partner with me to the Milan festival and we had at least four deals on the table for international distribution. It was the same old story though; my investor partner thought we should distribute it ourselves.

*You hadn't learned by now that this is where you hit them in the head with a pipe and hide the body?*

Yeah right, that's exactly it! I should have taken a two-by-four to him. I tried to explain to him that once we had sold the picture in a territory like Germany, we are in distribution knee deep because we can't try to sell it to another distributor. I did what he wanted me to do. I sold it to Germany for $60,000 and Japan for $40,000 so, right there, we had made our production costs back. Now there was no way we were going to get another distributor to pick it up for the rest of the world because the two major territories were already sold off.

The picture got a tremendous theatrical kick off in Germany. I don't know how they did with it in Japan, but the German version was fantastic. In dubbing, your actors become different people, but they did a great job. We had a strong lead actor for *Twister's Revenge*, but the girl — the lead actress — was very weak. That was bad casting. It did extremely well internationally, but I never closed a deal for theatrical distribution in the US.

*So* Twister's Revenge *wrapped up around 1988 or 1989?*

Yes. That's when disaster struck. I had a stroke. No one thought I was going to make it. The first thing my wife did was hire an attorney to represent us since I had no life insurance at the time. The attorney made the biggest mistake he possibly could have and put the wrong party into a bankruptcy. My wife and I had just returned from Europe selling *Twister's Revenge* and *Blood Harvest*, and we had spent our own money doing so. She told the attorney that we did not have any money personally because we had bank loans and maxed out credit cards from the pictures. He suggested that we put the studio into bankruptcy. The studio had assets of over $80,000, which with negatives were well over a million dollars. The liabilities were only about a fourth of that. So somehow this guy managed to put into bankruptcy a business that had three times the assets of its liabilities. I had no idea what was going on.

**Well Bill, that certainly sums up your extremely unique career in the motion picture industry. Is there anything else you would like to mention in closing?**

I don't like most of the work I did. The reason for that is not because the acting is amateurish or the effects aren't what they could have been. It's because it's not the work I wanted to do. I did it because I had to make a living. Once I got out of the industrial film business, it was very difficult to maintain clients while trying to do artistic ventures at the same time for the theatrical productions. While I was doing that whole series of films at the Shooting Ranch Studios in Gleason, I was always writing something totally different of major proportions that had nothing to do with horror, science fiction, monsters, etc. Every time I tried to sell one of those screenplays I would be told this was a love story or a comedy and I couldn't do that because I did horror and science fiction pictures. I realized I had become typecast, but I can't deny that it made me a living.

*Thank you very much for your time, Bill, and helping to get all of this down for posterity.*

It was my pleasure, ED. It's about time somebody did it.

# John A. Russo
## by Andrew J. Rausch

In 1968, long before the so-called "Independent Film Revolution," a group of unknown filmmakers from Pittsburgh set out to make a horror movie. Led by director George Romero and screenwriter John A. Russo, the team created a $114,000 masterpiece, *Night of the Living Dead*, about seven strangers who seek refuge from flesh-eating zombies. Despite its low budget, the black-and-white film was a huge success and has since continued to gain popularity, spawning countless imitations. Often touted as the most terrifying film ever made, the movie was listed by the National Film Registry as a classic in 1999. Respected film critic Leonard Maltin calls *Night of the Living Dead* the "touchstone modern horror film," warning, "Don't watch this alone!" The filmmakers then followed up their success with *There's Always Vanilla*.

Russo then redirected his talents toward writing books, churning out a number of successful novels, including *Hell's Creation*, *Living Things*, *The Awakening*, *Blood Sisters*, and *Limb to Limb*. A number of Russo's novels have been adapted into films, such as *Return of the Living Dead*, *Voodoo Dawn*, and *The Majorettes*, which Russo also produced and appears in. In addition, Russo is the author of *Making Movies: The Inside Guide to Independent Movie Production*, and has penned novelizations of *Night of the Living Dead* and Romero's *Day of the Dead*. In 1990, special effects wizard Tom Savini helmed a remake of *Night of the Living Dead*, for which Russo served as co-writer and producer.

Not only a successful novelist and screenwriter, Russo is also an accomplished filmmaker in his own right. In 1981, Russo made his directorial debut with *Midnight*, which he adapted from his own novel of the same title. Russo later directed the sequel *Midnight 2: Sex, Death, and Videotape*. That same year, Russo explored the theme of vampirism with *Heartstopper*. After making two films in 1996, *Scream Queens* and *Santa Claws*, Russo appeared in Academy Award-winning director Peter Werner's Emmy-nominated mini-series, *House of Frankenstein 1997*. Russo has also appeared as an actor in a number of other films, including *The Inheritor* and *I Married a Strange Person!*.

In 1999, Russo committed what many aficionados saw as the Cardinal Sin when he co-directed *Night of the Living Dead: 30th Anniversary Edition*, for which he shot a number of new scenes in black-and-white and integrated them into the 1968 classic. For this new edition, Russo excised nearly 15 minutes from the original film and added a new score. While some fans felt Russo's film was a great improvement over the original, others saw it as the ultimate blasphemy.

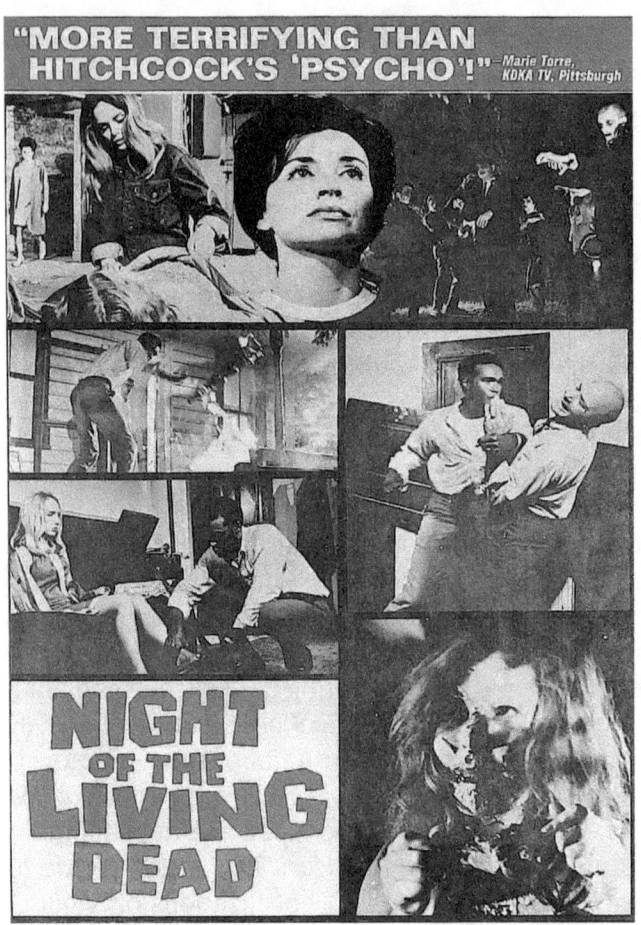

**Where did the concept for Night of the Living Dead come from?**

Well, George and I were both working on different ideas when we weren't doing commercial film. He and I were usually the main ones working on this stuff. He and I were both single at that time, so we spent most of our free time at the studio. We were the ones who would sleep on the floor and work all night. Whenever we weren't doing commercials, he'd go to one typewriter and I'd go to another one, and we'd work on story ideas. We had already decided we were going to do some kind of film.

So, I had a couple of pages already done that opened in the cemetery that actually had kids in ghoul masks. Our first idea was that a saucer would land. It was kind of an early *E.T.*, you know? The kids from outer space were gonna land and befriend these Earth kids, and they were gonna have a lot of powers that normal kids didn't have, running amok and causing havoc in the town. It was gonna be a sci-fi comedy, but we found out pretty quickly that we couldn't afford the special effects. Then George went away one weekend and wrote about half of a story, which opened in a cemetery. I had made the comment that cemeteries scare people and that would be a good way to open a film. I was working on another story about a kid who's running away from home. He's running through the woods and he steps through a pane of glass, like you use to grow hot-house tomatoes, only underneath is a rotting corpse. This was going to be about aliens who came to Earth in search of human flesh. George's story, which wasn't in screenplay form, got up to the point where it had the girl and it opened in the cemetery, and she was running from something and calling it a "thing." Well all liked the story, but I said to George, "Who are they and what do they do?" He didn't know! [Laughs.] So I said why not use my flesh-eating idea? It seems to me that they're people, so they must be dead people. Why not turn it around and make them flesh-eaters? He said that was good, so then we hashed that out. Then he said we couldn't show people coming up out of their graves, so I said, "Let's make them the recently dead. They're the only ones that can come back. That way we don't need all that special effects garbage." So, that's how it happened.

I took all the material and the ideas we had and wrote the script. By that time, I pretty much turned out to be the leader of the idea sessions. I don't know. It was like George was out of ideas or something, so people would get stumped and I'd say, "Well, here we've got Harry, and he's a coward. If something goes wrong during the escape attempt, he's not gonna stick. He's gonna try to save his own ass, so he'll probably board the damn door up when he wasn't supposed to." Things like that. So I took all these ideas and rewrote George's first ideas into screenplay form and then finished the second half of the screenplay.

Then George and I were at a friends' house, who was an investor, and George read the thing and said that something was bothering him. He didn't like it or something. Our friend read it and said, "There's nothing wrong with it. This is good." [Laughs.] So George said, "I know what's bothering me. There needs to be another siege before the ghouls finally overtake the people in the house. There needs to be another minor attack." So we wrote that in, and that was it. We changed things as we went. We changed the ending a little bit. We wanted to put Judy Ridley in there because she was good-looking, and we thought the film needed some sex

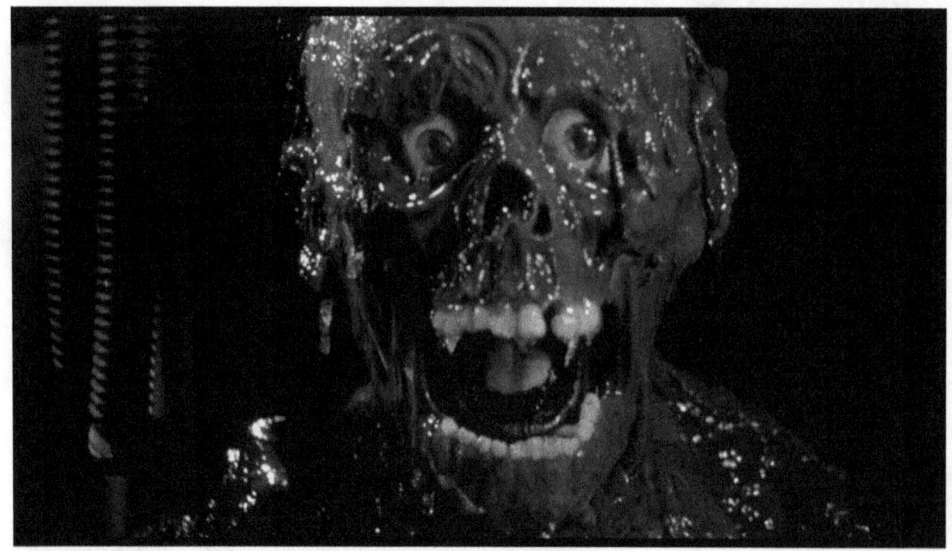
*One of the horrific zombies from John Russo's* Return of the Living Dead.

appeal because horror films had that at that time. It was originally written to be a guy. It was originally a cemetery caretaker who gets into the house, not the young couple. So we gave him a girlfriend and made him younger, just kind of writing her lines on the spur of the moment.

**One of the things that I find appealing about Night of the Living Dead is the combination of things you used to scare people. You had a touch of sci-fi, you had cannibalism, and the supernatural, all of which played upon people's natural fears of death.**

I saw every film that came to town when I was a kid. We had three movie theaters in a small town. I saw all the horror films. You always hoped you'd see something good, and I never really did until *Invasion of the Body Snatchers*. We wanted to make something better than these things with the rubber monsters that Hollywood was cranking out at the time. The zombie movies were my least favorites because the zombies didn't do anything but walk around looking stiff and dead. Once in a while they'd throw someone against the wall. They weren't frightening like Frankenstein or Dracula or any of that stuff. For that matter, neither were mummies. They were about in the same category. They weren't very scary.

What we did that really turned the trick was making them flesh-eaters. Now zombies were really terrifying because they ate human flesh, and they could turn you into one. Everyone's afraid of death, but now you could have a sort of life in death that nobody wanted. [Laughs.] I think another part of it was that using the recently dead tapped into those same feelings. You might bereave somebody who dies, but you don't really want to see them.

You don't really want to touch them. People are afraid of corpses, and it played off of those fears. I think it's a mistake what's gone on since then, where zombies are green and decayed and horrendous-looking. I guess that has its place, but I think it was much more frightening using the minimal makeup that we did. I think it touched some deeper vibes in people.

***Could you have ever imagined the film would become as big as it has over the years?***

Nobody could have imagined that because it's probably the only film there is that's been going on strong for 30 years. It's been in every format, and it's never been out of release. It's kind of a phenomenon in and of itself. If it would have had some kind of massive marketing campaign in the beginning, it probably would have been even bigger! I can't think of any other film that's had that run; not even any of the other famous horror films, like *Invasion of the Body Snatchers* or *Texas Chainsaw Massacre*.

***What is it about the horror genre that has drawn you back so many times as both a novelist and as a filmmaker?***

You can do good work in any genre. The thing about *Night of the Living Dead* is that the premise is outlandish, but we were true to the premise. The thing that makes it succeed is that once you've accepted the outlandish premise that the dead can rise and go after human flesh, we tried to make the people behave the way real people would behave in any kind of crisis. It's the same in *Stagecoach*; whenever you have a crisis, you have your cowards, you have your people with problems, and you have people who

can be more brave than others. You have the whole gamut, so that's what we tried to do.

As far as horror, you can work with any aspect of the human condition. It's kind of fun to play with the horror genre, too. You just take the old myths and give them new twists and play with people's minds.

**You recently directed** Night of the Living Dead: 30th Anniversary Edition, **which integrated newly-filmed scenes into the 30-year-old classic. What made you decide to do that?**

I'm a trustee of the corporation that made the movie, so if there comes a chance to colorize it or to do anything . . . I mean, I'm obligated to make as much money as I can for the shareholders. Beyond that, it was fun doing that. I wrote and directed the new scenes. Originally George was gonna direct it and we were gonna write it together, but he got involved with some other projects. When we got the money together and could finally do it, he was too busy.

But we had a great time doing it, and it looks absolutely terrific. It's really fun. This is no different from George Lucas going back and putting those scenes that he wanted to see in *Star Wars* back in there. It's really no different than a director's cut. What we tried to do were the things we had discussed 30 years ago but couldn't afford. One of the main things was that we desperately wanted an original score, and there was no way in hell we could afford that. We had to resort to library music, but now we've got a really good original score. We also wanted to explain why there were so many zombies surrounding this one little farmhouse out in the middle of nowhere. Where the hell did they come from? We never explained that, but now we have. You see that they were the patrons and waitresses and so on that worked at a diner.

The other thing is, the reason we didn't have featured zombies — there should have been continuing zombie characters, and with the exception of Bill Heinzman and myself, there weren't — was because we could never count on the same person showing up for two days in a row to be an extra. I ended up being the zombie that got the tire in the head because I was there working on the crew. It was four o'clock in the morning and everybody else had gone home. I figured, well, I'll get into the goddamned makeup and still load magazines. Now we have featured zombie characters.

Everything integrates perfectly. Plus, we were able to fix a lot of things. The famous jump cut is gone now. Bill Heinzman came up with a way to edit that gets rid of that. There's been criticism from people on the Internet who don't know anything about this. They *can't* know anything about it because they haven't seen it yet. But they're pissing and moaning that I should have my ass kicked and all that because we shortened the movie!

Oh, my God! Well, if it was their movie and they had a chance to do this, they'd fall all over themselves to get to a camera. We judiciously shortened things, you know? If you just shave a few seconds off of the shots . . . You don't even miss those few seconds, but it gives you time to add another key scene or character. This is just common practice. This is how you shave time off of anything. You don't even miss any of the stuff we took out. It's not like anything was devastated. It's all there, plus you get all this new stuff that's a lot of fun. It's entertaining as hell.

**Do you think there are any subject matters that should be taboo for a filmmaker, or do you think the sky is the limit?**

No, I don't think anything should be taboo. It just depends on the handling of it. We need to learn about everything under the sun. It's just a question of taste, restraint, and manners.

**Do you think there is a place for these films like Faces of Death?**

Oh, there's a place for it . . . [Laughs.] Right up the ass of the person who distributed it!

# Ray Dennis Steckler
## by ED Tucker

**EDITOR'S NOTE:** *Ray Dennis Steckler made his directorial debut with* Wild Guitar. *He then directed the grindhouse classic* The Incredibly Strange Creatures Who Stopped Living and Became Mixed-Up Zombies!!?. *Steckler took the film on the road and it played successfully for a number of years with various titles, including* The Teenage Psycho Meets Bloody Mary *and* Diabolical Dr. Voodoo. *Steckler is also known for the serial killer film* The Thrill Killers, *which he starred in himself. Other notable titles include* Body Fever, Blood Shack, *and* The Hollywood Strangler Meets the Skid Row Slasher. *Steckler passed away in 2009 at the age of 70.*

Ray Dennis Steckler was an incredibly genial man and as gracious a host as anyone could ask for. To say that I interviewed Ray would be a misstatement. Ray Dennis Steckler interviewed himself or, if anything, he interviewed me! He was highly opinionated about his profession but shared these opinions with such an air of honesty and a lack of pretension that it was hard not to get caught in his jet stream of consciousness. To escape from the greed, corruption, and fakery of Hollywood, Steckler moved to Las Vegas in the 1970s and made his home and films in a town best known for its towering and abundant casinos. According to Steckler, he left because he couldn't find a place to park in Hollywood, and by the time this interview took place it was getting that way in Vegas!

It is to the south of this Technicolor nightmare and in the shadow of a far more impressive mountain range that Steckler ran his last remaining video store. The other stores were sold off to consolidate his businesses when health problems finally slowed him down. Despite the slower pace, Ray Steckler remained active right up until his death in January of 2009. I was honored to know Ray and proud to call him my friend.

The interview you are about to read was originally conducted over several sessions in March 2001 and updated in April of 2004.

**Ray, I think by now most people are familiar with your more famous pictures like** The Incredibly Strange Creatures Who Stopped Living and Became Mixed Up Zombies **and** The Thrill Killers. **I would like to talk about some of your lesser known productions including some of the more recent ones. The first film you ever made was the short** Goof on the Loose **in 1959, correct?**

Interviewer ED Tucker with the late Ray Dennis Steckler.

Yes, *Goof on the Loose* was the first film I ever did entirely by myself. I had always been a big fan of the silent comedians like Buster Keaton. He was a tremendously physical comedian. He made some incredible films like *The General*, but towards the end of his career he had to make some terrible films just to stay alive.

**He was in a number of films for AIP including some of the "beach party" movies. It always amazed me because he was old and not a real match for these kinds of films. They would give him bad parts and only have him on screen for about 10 minutes and he would still steal the show.**

He never made any money because he didn't own the rights to his films like Charlie Chaplin did. He was at the mercy of the studios and just trying to stay alive and that was what they did to him. Towards the end he worked for MGM and they paired him with Jimmy Durante. Buster Keaton was a very physical and mobile comedian, where Durante was dependent on dialogue. I guess they were pushing Durante because he'd had some recent success on Broadway, but they were just mismatched.

**Keaton was still trying to make silent films, even then.**

Good for him. He was the last. Nobody has the guts to do that anymore. Nobody except me. No one else would have tried to do what I just did with *Summer Fun*.

***In your acting career, did you limit yourself to just working in your own pictures? I know you had a brief cameo in the film*** Eegah! ***for Arch Hall, but did you do anything besides that for anyone else?***

I did a few other parts. I was in *Las Vegas Weekend* and a few other pictures, but they were for friends. It's not like I went out and worked for anybody. I never solicited a movie role in my life. I was asked to do *The Incredible Two-Headed Transplant*, but I saw the make-up and told them you'd have to be a fool to do this; it will haunt you the rest of your life. Bruce Dern was in it.

***Bruce Dern, Pat Priest from The Munsters, and Casey Kasem.***

I don't know if that was a mistake or not. I don't think so. The film was directed by Anthony Lanza, who was my editor on *Wild Guitar*. He was a very interesting and talented guy. He edited some of *Strange Creatures* for me, too. He did the scene at the end of the chase down the beach, which was really well edited with the rocks and the water and the splashing. When I took a look at it it was just edited terribly. I asked him what happened and he said there was nothing there. I went through all the trims and I reedited the whole scene that day, and I'm glad I did because I love that chase scene at the end.

I didn't have any faith in Anthony Lanza after that as an editor, but I think he would make a competent director in the conventional sense. I never saw *The Incredible Two-Headed Transplant*. I don't know what happened to him after that, but I felt he had the ability to go a long way.

***I saw that film originally at a drive-in in Jacksonville, Florida, on a double feature with*** Frankenstein Conquers the World. ***I even have a poster for it, but I never realized Anthony Lanza directed it.***

This is what I am getting at. People remember that film, but no one remembers who directed it. People see my films and they remember my name. I am not being immodest about this, but they remember my name and more. I even get accused of doing films I never made. *The Incredible Two-Headed Transplant* wasn't Anthony Lanza's film. He directed it, but he was doing it for someone else. The type of person who is going to pick up a camera and make his own film from start to finish is the type of person who will get destroyed in Hollywood.

***Hollywood rewards the person who is just doing a job?***

You have to understand something about Hollywood through the years. I have read a lot about it, and let's just say I am well-versed in it. What is Hollywood? Is it a town? Is it a group of people? Is it a figment of your imagination? What is Hollywood really? Hollywood is a place where when they don't need you anymore, that's it. They have the motion picture home now, thank God, to save some of these people. In Hollywood you can work for five or 10 years, and then what? Do you go out and pump gas? Actors can be on a hit television series for three or five years, and then it's over. During that time maybe they made some enemies or said the wrong thing and suddenly no one wants them.

I worked with a number of the major studios. I even had an office for a while at MGM. I worked with a number of key players including Harold Robbins. They all wanted to meet me, but no one ever wanted to do anything with me. I was typed as a cameraman. I started off as a cameraman and I worked as a cameraman. I did the *Wild World of Sports*, I did a series called *The Professionals*. I filmed over 100 commercials. I did all these things as a cameraman but it never lead to another job as a director. I had to go home and put money in a sock until I had enough saved up to start another picture.

**So you gave up on Hollywood?**

By the time I did *Body Fever*, I had found myself at a point in my life where I just decided to have some fun. I didn't really care anymore; the damage from Hollywood had been done. As I am sure you know, I didn't start out acting in that picture but I ended up acting in it. I didn't have enough money to do that picture correctly, but I finished it. The very first day on the set in San Pedro, the assistant cameraman had $25,000 worth of lenses and he took his eye off them and someone walked away with the case. We had one lens left to shoot that day and it was a bad lens!

**Let's jump forward a few years to my personal favorite of yours, The Lemon Grove Kids Meet the Monsters. It was your tribute to the films of the Bowery Boys.**

Yes. That is exactly what it was intended to be — a tribute.

**You did three short films in the series. What order were they filmed in?**

*The Not So Great Race* was the first one.

**[Laughs.] Actually that was The Great Race.**

[Laughs.] *The Lemon Grove Kids Meet the Green Grasshopper and His Vampire Lady* was second, and *The Lemon Grove Kids Go Hollywood* was the third one.

**It was in between the second and the third films that you were contacted by Huntz Hall.**

His wife threatened to sue me if I wore the baseball hat again. So I didn't wear the hat in the third one because I didn't want to have any problems. I almost made a movie with him. We talked about it, but he wanted too much money. A lot of people say I make movies about other movies and that might be true to an extent. Movies were my escapism as a child and I wanted to recreate the films that I liked to go see the best that I could. I think we did a wonderful job on *The Lemon Grove Kids* and I don't think we came that close to the Bowery Boys, but, let's face it, a lot of people think we did. If nothing else, we did the East Side Kids/Bowery Boys in color, and even they never did that!

**Was The Lemon Grove Kids *originally intended as a series of vignettes?***

No. When we made *The Great Race* in 1967 it was intended to be a feature. I still have so much footage from that it's incredible. All we knew is that we wanted to make a Bowery Boys movie but we didn't know what direction we wanted to go in and we didn't have any money to do it with. I just decided at some point that there wasn't enough there to make a feature. I could have done it, and I probably still could with all the footage I have. If I went back now and edited that into a feature, it would look nothing like the one that ended up on the screen. I just love *The Lemon Grove Kids*, even to this day. I did a fourth one but never finished it.

**Do you recall the plot of the fourth film?**

It's a secret! It would complete the trilogy!

**[Laughs.] The four film trilogy!**

[Laughs.] Yes, Ray Steckler's four film trilogy. I would love to put that on the video box cover! Let me tell you, there is a fourth film there.

**So after you filmed The Great Race, *you decided to scrap the idea of a feature and go with shorts instead?***

I just decided to do the first one as a short and see if we could sell the idea. We tried to sell it as a television pilot but no one was interested in it. They thought with the dialogue looping it was too amateurish. When it got out to the theaters, no one gave a darn about that. They didn't care if it was looped or not; they liked what they saw. I was in the theaters when it played, and everybody loved them! I put the Green Grasshopper one first and then added footage to the end of *The Great Race* with all the thunder and lightning. That was in part with the mummy so they could have the guy in the mummy costume come out in the theater.

**The live section was done at the end of the third segment in the film?**

No, there were only two segments in the film. *Go Hollywood* was never shown in the theaters — that only came out on video. The film only ran about an hour in theaters. There were times when we actually rented a Bowery Boys film to play with it.

**Was The Great Race *the last film you did with George Morgan?***

Yes. After that I went with Keith A. Wester. He had done the sound for me on *Rat Pfink and Boo Boo*. He was nominated for six Academy Awards for Best Sound, but he never won. The most recent was *A Perfect Storm*. He passed away recently.

**He also played Marvin Marvin in The Lemon Grove Kids.**

He was Marvin Marvin in the first two and Swami Marvin in *Go Hollywood*. If I was to re-release the film I could say "starring Keith A. Wester, six-time Academy Award nominee"! He was very good in *The Lemon Grove Kids*, and he's done a lot of other things, too.

**You finished the final segment of The Lemon Grove Kids in 1969. How long after this was the film released to theaters?**

I have to tell you, it was not very long at all. A fellow named Joe Karston had been doing road shows of my pictures since 1966 or 1967. He did *The Incredibly Strange Creatures* (retitled *The Teenage Psycho Meets Bloody Mary*) and then *The Thrill Killers* (retitled *The Maniacs are Loose*). He came to me after that and said, "What have you got?" I showed him The Lemon Grove Kids and he said that would be good for matinee shows. A lot of theaters back then enjoyed booking a matinee show just for Saturdays.

**How many years did that play as a matinee?**

That played for about five or six years. I think it all washed out about 1975 or 1976.

**That played longer than I realized. You had a theater employee dressed as a mummy run through audiences when this film played. What did you have for the others?**

When they did *The Thrill Killers* they dressed like the Cash Flagg character. When they did *Strange Creatures* they had people dressed like the zombies except for the first six months when I went on tour with the film. Then for *The Lemon Grove Kids* they did the mummy.

**Did you have to go back and film inserts for the mummy section?**

Yes. There was originally a mummy in *The Great Race* played by Bob Burns who also played Kogar the gorilla for me in *Rat Pfink*. Bob came back and did the mummy for me again in the insert footage. There was a girl in that scene with the mummy who had played a dancer in The Incredibly Strange Creatures. Her name was Cindy Shea and she was best friends with Carolyn Brandt from the time we moved to Hollywood. She was in the hospital with cancer and did not have long to live. She knew we were shooting that day and she actually left the hospital — she walked out.

Somehow she got there and she walked up that big hill. I can still remember seeing her and I don't know how she did it. She just said, "I want to be part of your movie, please. Just do something." I don't know if I would have shot that scene in the same way if she hadn't shown up when she did. She was just wonderful. Less than a week later she was gone, and I never really got over that. Someone wanted to be in one of my pictures that much.

**Didn't Ron Haydock play Rat Pfink again in that same segment?**
Yes, and he was also the guitar player in *The Great Race*.

**I picked up a really cool CD called *99 Chicks* by Ron Haydock & the Boppers that has Rat Phink tracks on it. Are you familiar with that?**
That's the one on Norton Records.

**Right. There are some great photos in the CD booklet, too.**

Those came from me. They contacted me and I sent them some items on Ron for the booklet.

**There is one I have never seen before of him on the hood of a car holding two masks. What are they from?**

One is the head from *Thrill Killers* that rolls down the stairs. I'm not sure about the other.

**How about the shot of Ron performing on stage dressed as Rat Phink?**

That is from the tour we did to promote the film. We went around to supermarkets with Ron dressed as Rat Pfink and another guy doing Boo Boo because Titus Mode was not available. It was also me. Carolyn Brandt, who was my wife at the time, and my 81-year-old grandfather. We went all over the place trying to drum up interest in the film. We shot some color film of those appearances that I put on the end of the *Rat Pfink* video.

**There is also a picture in the booklet of a pulp novel called Caged Lust. It looks like Bill Ward-style artwork on the cover and it is credited to Vin Saxon. Is that for real?**

Oh yeah. Vin Saxon was, of course, Ron Haydock. He must have written 50 of those things. One was called *Ape Rape*. They were very strange.

**Well, with a title like Ape Rape I'm not surprised.**

You have to understand, that was how Ron made a living towards the end of his life. They would pay him $500 to write one of these things. The books are very rare now because they only printed about 20,000 of them to begin with. I think Norton must have a whole collection of these things somewhere. They came to me looking for one of his titles, but I didn't even have it. Ron Haydock made movies for me, but no one else would give him a chance. I not only gave him a chance, I hocked my house to make those movies and to record those songs because I believed in him. Then he got screwed up with depression a couple of times, thinking that no one cared about him. I cared about him. I say this, if you go through your whole life and you only have one person that cares about you, who is willing to sacrifice for you, then you are well ahead of the game. That's honestly what I believe, and when Ron killed himself there was no reason for him to do that except he felt he wasn't wanted.

**Hold on — did Ron kill himself? I thought he died in a car accident hitchhiking back to California from visiting you in Vegas?**

It wasn't an accident. I had given him a plane ticket, too, but he wouldn't use it. I could talk about the whole story, but I don't want it changed. If enough people want to hear about it, I'll tell you. It's not really a story that puts Ron Haydock down. He was my best friend. I think my career almost came to a halt when he died.

***Whatever happened to Mike Kannon who played Slug in* The Lemon Grove Kids? *I thought he was great in the Leo Gorcey part.***

He became a security guard at the Romane headquarters of Howard Hughes. He was the one who got tied up when Hughes was robbed and they got all his papers. He also acted in *The Getaway* with Steve McQueen. He was a fine actor.

***One of your later films actually takes its title from a character in* The Lemon Grove Kids. *How did you come up with the idea of* The Chooper?**

Herb Robins played the character in the Green Grasshopper segment and that's what he did, he went "choop, choop, choop, choop, choop." So he became *The Chooper*.

***[Laughs.] That's it? That's all there was to it? I saw a video box for the film one time and they had this elaborate definition of how a Chooper was a legendary evil spirit!***

Nah! Whatever we had, that was what we made a movie with. I said, "Hey, we've still got a Chooper suit," so Ron became The Chooper. It didn't even fit him. It was too small. My whole philosophy is when it's someone else's money you're spending, that's a whole different ballgame than when it's your own. Before you make a movie you look around and see what you have, not what you want to go get. Think about all the things you don't have to spend money for and then write your story around them, because now you've saved $20,000. If you look at my films you will see the same things here and there because if it was still good, fine, then we used it again.

***Was* The Chooper *released to theaters?***

It played in one theater in Denver, Colorado, but was really just straight to video.

***So you were eligible for the Academy Awards?***

[Laughs.] Yes, that's a good line!

***Right after* The Chooper *you did another film called* Bloody Jack *that so far remains unreleased.***

Yes. That had Herb Robins, Carolyn Brandt, and myself in it. It was a basic serial killer plot. Charlie Smith returns and all the women he knows starts to get killed. This guy is obsessed with Charlie Smith but rather than kill him he kills all his friends. It was great stuff. It was shot on 16mm with sync sound and everything. It could still be saved. It needs to be edited and scored. We had a flood a while back and the film went into storage and I haven't done anything with it since.

***How do you have a flood in Nevada?***

Well, the guy next door was putting in a barbershop and he did his own plumbing. He was gone and a pipe blew. We couldn't get in, we couldn't find the landlord, and the water came in here fast! I had to get the stuff I could save out of here fast and it all went into storage unmarked.

**So Bloody Jack was your last film until The Hollywood Strangler Meets the Skid Row Slasher in 1979?**

Yes. Even though the setting was Hollywood, we filmed most of it in Las Vegas and no one realized it. Then we did *The Las Vegas Serial Killer*. A third one was shot but Pierre Agostino, who played the killer, didn't want to do it. He said he didn't want to come back for a third time, and he never came back. I think we were going to call it *The Return of the Hollywood Strangler*. There is also a fourth one we shot that still needs to be edited called *The Son of the Hollywood Strangler*. I shot the whole thing on 16mm and never put it together. Then I took the two guys from *The Las Vegas Serial Killer* and made a movie called *The Las Vegas Thrill Killers*. That was around 1993.

**So there was about a four year gap between that and your most recent film Summer Fun. How did that one come about?**

Well, that actually started as an idea Ron Haydock and I had in the sixties for a film about these characters called Flip and Flop. Ron said, "Let's do this film called *Flip and Flop*." Of course I would play Flop so he could get top billing! We would have played two detectives and we get hired for this case. The whole key to it is they say we have to go to Africa. We look at each other and say, "Okay," and in the next cut we're in Africa! I would have loved to have done that, but we never got around to it. We actually shot part of another jungle picture with Ron and Carolyn and myself. We had Bob Burns in the gorilla costume and he finds a little girl in a plane wreck. We got to Africa to find this girl who is now grown up. We shot all the footage, and I still have it, but we never made the movie.

**So the Flip and Flop characters got carried over into Summer Fun?**

Only the names, really. The characters are not the same. We had Herb Robins in that and he got a lot of people involved from around Lake Tahoe. We brought some of the cast with us from Las Vegas and, of course, my daughter Bailey is in it. One girl in the film was Miss Mississippi and she came in the finals of the Miss America contest. She was just in the lead of one of the new *Power Rangers* shows.

**I'd rather be in one of your films any day! Speaking of cheesy science fiction shows, what do you think about your films being shown on Mystery Science Theater 3000?**

I think it's just disgusting. I think the people that wrote that should be ashamed of some of the things they said. If they want to poke fun at my films, that's fine. We went out and made a movie, and they have a right to say what they think about it, but some of the things they said in that show were just disgusting. I don't even like to talk about it because it upsets me so much. They never had the rights from me to show the pictures.

The guys that do that show just have no respect for what a filmmaker goes through with very little money. You give up a lot to make a movie like *Strange Creatures* — time and money. I did not need the kind of racist, sexist, and even anti-Semitic remarks those guys made. I just think they were wrong to do it. I hope they made a lot of money off that and then spent it unwisely. The show is off the air now, so it really doesn't matter.

Let me ask you something — have you ever heard me knock anyone before?

*No, I can honestly say in anything I have read or seen about you, you have never said an unkind word about anyone. I can also add that I know firsthand from talking with other filmmakers that you are not alone in your sentiments towards that show. Fortunately* Mystery Science Theater 3000 *has been cancelled and that is all in the past. Let's talk about your future now. You have your website up and running. Do you have plans to expand it?*

Yes. I have a lot of stuff to put up on that. I have some reproduction lobby cards that I need to get on there. It isn't doing that well and I'm not really sure why. I still go on tour, and I sell a lot of stuff that way. I'm also selling some films on eBay.

***Last time we spoke you were working on a new film. Is that still in production?***

Yes. Now I am calling it *Steckler's Eleven*, and I am going to get 11 people that I worked with in the past back together. I found Mike Kannon; he's retired and living in an apartment in Hollywood. I talked to him on the phone and he seemed a little tired, but he is 70-years-old or close to it. I have Robert Blair who played the lead in *Wild Ones on Wheels*, Jim Bowie from *Rat Pfink*, and Herb Robins from *The Thrill Killers*. John Waite, who was in *Summer Fun*, is in it, too. I may get Carolyn Brandt to be in it just to make it to 11.

***You have a tape out now of two unreleased films,* Face of Evil *and* Slashed. *Where do these fit into the Ray Dennis Steckler filmography?***

I started a film with an actor friend of mine named Will Long. About three or four days into the film, he caught hepatitis, and within a few days he had died. It just shocked me and I had to put the film aside. Fortunately I had shot a scene from the beginning, a scene from the middle, and a scene from the end of the film. So I had those but nothing else. A few years later I started another film with a girlfriend, a stripper named Lovie Goldmine. I started making a slasher movie with her and about 50 percent of the way through the film she told me she had to leave town immediately. She took her kids and disappeared, and I never heard from her again. She was a wonderful person. I hope she sees this and contacts me.

I didn't have the ending filmed, so I had to fake it with Carolyn Brandt playing her part. I crossed footage between the two films. It was an experiment, so in both movies you see some of the same footage. It really blows your mind. I made 25 copies of these films on video and then I destroyed the master.

***Two of your films,* Rat Pfink and Boo Boo *and* The Lemon Grove Kids Meet the Monsters *have recently been released on DVD by Media Blasters. Was there any reason these two were chosen first instead of your more well known films like* The Thrill Killers *or* Incredibly Strange Creatures? *Aside from the fact that these two are my favorites that is!***

I did that. I did it to build up momentum. I wanted to get people interested and then work my way up to the bigger pictures. *Blood Shack* is coming out next. The DVD will have both versions of the film, *Blood Shack* and *The Chooper*. I do the commentary on *Blood Shack* and Joe Bob Briggs does the commentary on *The Chooper*. The DVD will also contain a special interview with Carolyn Brandt. *Hollywood Strangler Meets the Skid Row Slasher* will be next. It's already done. I just recorded the commentary last week. After that I will probably have them put out *Body Fever* and *Creatures*.

**Why did they choose to use a recreated photo for the cover of the** Rat Pfink *DVD instead of the original still or artwork?*

That was Media Blasters' decision and I don't really know why they did that. They did a much better job with *The Lemon Grove Kids*, and I am really happy with the way that turned out. I let them handle the marketing and I just supply the material.

**You have put together a lot of great interview tapes of yourself with all kinds of interesting rare footage. Do you plan to migrate those over to DVD?**

Probably not, because the quality really isn't there. These are mostly things people grab at shows and the lighting is bad, the sound is bad.

**Not even a greatest hits type DVD?**

Well, I have thought about putting all the shows together in a DVD box set for my fans at a price they could live with.

**When** The Thrill Killers *is released on DVD, will it have the alternate version of* The Maniacs are Loose *included?*

That is something we are talking about right now. We are also talking a possible re-release to the theaters to coincide with the DVD release and also a possible sequel. My friend Louie Esposito, who wrote the novel *Mafia Cop*, is working on the story. Mad Dog Click gets out of jail 40 years later and he's now an old man. His days of murder are over and he retires to the small town of Reading, Pennsylvania. He tries to put his life back together, which is not easy to do after being in jail for 40 years. A relative of one of his victims is now a homicide detective who decides to frame him for murder. So Mad Dog Click is going to get framed for a murder he did not commit. Things are going to get more interesting from there, but that is the thread of the idea. If the DVDs sell well enough and there is enough interest, they may be willing to do a sequel.

**So if enough people contact Media Blasters, they will do a sequel to** The Thrill Killers?

Have people contact Media Blasters and let them know that they would like to see the sequel to *The Thrill Killers* called *Mad Dog Click*, starring me. Media Blasters is considering doing it, but I want people to give them some input. Let Media Blasters know that we want Cash Flagg back. We want Cash! I want cash, too, but that's beside the point!

**I can't wait to see it! Thanks for your time, Ray. It's been a pleasure.**

Mine too. Thanks.

# Acknowledgments

Bryan Layne's interview with Charles Band first appeared as "Interview with Charles Band," Gutmunchers (**Gutmunchers.com**). It appears by permission of the author.

Mike White's interview with Greydon Clark first appeared as "Shades of Greydon Clark," *Cashiers du Cinemart*, issue 14, 2002. It appears by permission of the author.

Andrew J. Rausch's interview with Larry Cohen first appeared in the book *Reflections on Blaxploitation*, Scarecrow Press, Inc., 2009. It appears by permission of Scarecrow Press, Inc.

Andrew J. Rausch's interview with Roger Corman first appeared as "Roger Corman on *The Blair Witch Project* and Why *Mean Streets* Would Have Made a Great Blaxploitation Film," *Images*, issue nine, 2000. It appears by permission of the author.

Nathaniel Thompson's interview with David F. Friedman first appeared as "Step Right Up!: The Cinematic Sideshows of David F. Friedman," Mondo Digital (**Mondo-Digital.com**). It appears by permission of the author.

Colleen Wanglund's interview with Frank Henlotter first appeared as "Interview with *Basket Case* Director Frank Henlotter," MoreHorror.com. It appears by permission of Seth Metoyer, **MoreHorror.com**.

Chris Watson's interview with Jack Hill first appeared in the book *Reflections on Blaxploitation*, Scarecrow Press, Inc., 2009. It appears by permission of Scarecrow Press, Inc.

Andrew Leavold's interview with Alejandro Jodorowsky first appeared as "Alejandro Jodorowsky Interview," *Rave Magazine*, June 2008. It appears by permission of the author.

David Carroll and Kyla Ward's interview with Lloyd Kaufman first appeared as "Holy Shit! What Is All This Green Stuff?," *Tabula Rasa*, issue one, 1994. It appears by permission of David Carroll.

Andrew J. Rausch's interview with Herschell Gordon Lewis first appeared in the book *Fifty Filmmakers: Conversations with Directors from Roger Avary to Steven Zaillian*, McFarland & Company, Inc., 2008. It appears by permission of McFarland & Company, Inc.

Devin Faraci's interview with William Lustig first appeared as "The Badass Interview: William Lustig," Badass Digest (**badassdigest.com**), February 7, 2011. It appears by permission of the author.

Sandra Gin Yep and Mike Carroll's interview with Russ Meyer has never appeared in print before. It appears by permission of Mike Carroll.

Andrew Leavold's interview with Ted V. Mikels first appeared in longer form as "King of the Astro-Zombies: Ted V. Mikels Interviewed," *Trash Confidential*, 2002. It appears by permission of the author.

ED Tucker's interview with Bill Rebane has never appeared in print before. It appears by permission of the author.

Andrew J. Rausch's interview with John A. Russo first appeared in the book *Fifty Filmmakers: Conversations with Directors from Roger Avary to Steven Zaillian*, McFarland & Company, Inc., 2008. It appears by permission of McFarland & Company, Inc.

ED Tucker's interview with Ray Dennis Steckler first appeared in a slightly different form as "The Incredibly Strange Creatures Who Talked Movies and Became the Mixed-Up Ray Dennis Steckler Interview," **crazedfanboy.com**. It appears by permission of the author.

# Index

Across 110th Street 28
Adamson, Al 19, 20-21
*Adult Story of Jekyll & Hyde, The* 52
Agostino, Pierre 159
*Alpha Incident* 132
*American Gangster* 27
*American Werewolf in London* 46
*Angel of Vengeance* 114
*Angel's Brigade* 20, 22, 23
*Angel's Revenge* 20
*Ape Rape* 156
*Apocalypse Now* 79
*Apollo 13* 37
Argento, Dario 99
Arkoff, Sam 27, 29, 71, 122
*Astro-Zombies* 109, 118
*The Awakening* 141
Babb, Kroger 44
*The Babysitter Murders* 14
*Bad Biology* 55, 57
*The Bad Bunch* 21
Baker, Joe Don 21-22
Balodis, Ilze 58
Band, Albert 11, 13
Band, Charles 11-8
*Basket Case* 47, 55, 56, 57-60, 62, 63
*Basket Case 2*, 61
*Basket Case 3: The Progeny* 61
*Battle Beyond the Stars* 40
Bava, Mario 46
*Bayou* 43
*Because of Eve* 44
*Bell, Bare and Beautiful* 45
Bell, Virginia 45
Benissimo, Salvator 19
*Best Seller* 25
*Beyond the Valley of the Dolls* 101, 103, 106
*The Big Bird Cage* 65, 68
*The Big Doll House* 37, 65, 68, 71
*Black Caesar* 25, 26-29, 30, 31, 32, 33, 34
*Black Dynamite* 4
Black, Karen 49
*The Black Klansman* 114, 116, 118
*Black Love* 89
*Black Shampoo* 19-20, 21, 22, 23
*Black Sunday* 46
*Black Snake Moan* 4
Blair, Robert 160
*The Blair Witch Project* 38-39
Blakely, Susan 22
Blasco, Joe 50
*Blood Feast* 43, 45, 46-47, 49, 50, 89, 90, 91
*Blood Feast 2: All U Can Eat* 43, 47, 90
*Blood Harvest* 137, 139
*Blood Orgy of the She-Devils* 109

*Blood Shack* 149, 160
*Blood Sisters* 141
*Bloody Jack* 158
Bobbitt, Charles 33-34
Bodkin, Tain 129
*Body Fever* 149, 152, 160
Bogdanovich, Peter 40
*Bone* 25, 27
Bonner, Bill 19
*Boss Nigger* 7
Bowers, Bill 42
*Bowery Boys* 152
Bowie, Jim 161
*Boxcar Bertha* 41
*Brain Damage* 55, 59, 61
*Branded* 26
Brandt, Carolyn 157, 161
*Brigadoon* 47
Briggs, Joe Bob 89, 160
Brodie, Kevin 131
Brodie, Steve 129, 131
Brown, James 33-34
Brown, Peter 70
Bunuel, Luis 46, 75
*Burn, Coffy, Burn* 70
Burns, Bob 154
Burzynski, Leszek 137
*But Charlie, I Never Played Volleyball* 52
*The Calling* 13
*Caged Heat* 39
*Caged Lust* 156
Cagney, James 27
Cameron, James 37, 40-41
Capra, Frank 121
Carpenter, John 14-15
*Cellular* 25
Chaplin, Charles 79, 150
*Charlie's Angels* 114
Chase, Brandon 129, 130
*The Chooper* 157, 160
*Chopper Chicks in Zombie Town* 83, 84
Christ, Jesus 74, 75, 106
*Citizen Kane* 52
Clark, Greydon 19-23
*Class of Nuke 'Em High* 79, 81
*Class of Nuke 'Em High III* 81, 83, 84
Cocteau, Jean 75
*Coffy* 65, 66, 68, 69, 70, 71
Cohen, Larry 3, 25-35, 100
Cole, Jackie 20
*Color Me Blood Red* 43, 48, 49, 50, 89
Connors, Chuck 14
Coppola, Francis Ford 37, 39, 42, 65
Corman, Roger 37-42, 65, 67, 82, 123
*The Corpse Grinders* 109, 115, 116

Costner, Kevin 85, 88
Cotton, Joseph 14
Cromreiter, Tony 129
*Cruising* 97
*The Crying Game* 82
Cundey, Dean 23
Cunningham, Sean 46
Curtis, Tony 22
Da Vinci, Leonardo 75
*Dahmer vs. Gacy* 7
*Dangerous Worry Dolls* 16, 18
Daniels, John 19
*Dance Craze* 122
*Dance Macabre* 23
Dante, Joe 39, 41
*Dark Future* 23
*Daughter of the Sun* 49
David, Alan 121
Davis, Andrew 14
Davis Jr., Sammy 25, 27
*Day of the Dead* 141
*Dead Dudes in the House* 85
*Death Race 2000* 38
*Death Wish* 96
*Def By Temptation* 83, 85
*The Defilers* 49
*Dementia 13* 37, 39, 65
DeMille, Cecil B. 91
Demme, Jonathan 39, 40
*Demons of Ludlow* 135-6
Dequina, Mike 37
Dern, Bruce 151
*The Devil's Rejects* 4
*Diabolical Dr. Voodoo* 149
*Die Hard* 88
*Direct Mail Copy That Sells!* 89
*The Doll Squad* 109, 114
*Dollman vs. Demonic Toys* 11
DoQui, Robert 69
*Dracula vs. Frankenstein* 19
*Dune* 75
Durante, Jimmy 150
*Dwarfsploitation* 7
Dyke, William 129
E.C. Comics 46
*E.T.* 143
Easton, Robert 129, 130, 131
Eastwood, Clint 14
*Easy Rider* 21
Edmonds, Don 51
*Eegah!* 150
*El Condor* 25
*El Topo* 73, 74, 75, 76
*Enchanted April* 82
*The Erotic Adventures of Zorro* 43, 50, 52
Esper, Dwain 43, 44
Esposito, Louie 161
*Evil Ever After* 7

*Face of Evil* 160
*Faces of Death* 147
Faithfull, Marianne 107
*The Fakers* 20
Fanaka, Jamaa 7
*Fando and Lis* 74, 75
*Faster, Pussycat! Kill! Kill!* 101, 102
Fetchit, Stepin 69
*Film Alchemy* 4
*Final Justice* 22
*A Fistful of Dollars* 14
*The Forbidden Dance* 19, 23
*Forbidden Love* 44
Ford, John 79
Forster, William 95
*Foxy Brown* 65, 69, 70, 71
Franco, Jesus 46
*Frankenhooker* 55, 61
*Frankenstein Conquers the World* 151
*Freaks* 44
*Friday the 13th* 45
Friedman, David F. 43-53
*The Fugitive* 14
Fulci, Lucio 99
*The Game* 136
Garris, Mick 6
Garroni, Andy 97
Gavin, Erica 108
*The General* 150
Gertz, Elmer 103
*The Getaway* 157
*Ghoulies* 11, 12, 18
*The Giant Spider Invasion* 121, 129-31, 132, 136
*Gift from a Red Planet* 132
Gillet, Tom 129
*Girl in Gold Boots* 117
*Girl on a Motorcycle* 107
*The Girl, the Body and the Pill* 91
*God Told Me To* 25
*The Godfather Part II* 37, 42
Golan, Menachem 23
Goldmine, Lovie 160
*Gone with the Wind* 50
Gordon, Larry 70
*The Gore Gore Girls* 89
Graham, Gloria 14
*The Great Race* 152, 153, 154, 155
Grier, Pam 28, 65, 66, 68, 70
*Grindhouse* 3, 6
Hahn, Jessica 103
Haig, Sid 65, 68
Hale, Alan 129
Hale, Barbara 129, 131
Hall, Huntz 152
*Halloween* 15, 45, 89
Harris, Julius 32
Hauser, Wings 22
Haydock, Ron 155, 158

Hefner, Hugh 103
Heinzman, William 146
*Hell Up in Harlem* 25, 30, 32, 33, 34
*Hell's Bloody Devils* 19
*Hell's Creation* 141
Hellman, Monte 40
*Hellride* 4
Hendry, Gloria 31, 32
Henenlotter, Frank 47, 55-63
Henriksen, Lance 14
*Henry and June* 106
*Herschell Gordon Lewis: The Godfather of Gore* 55
Herz, Michael 79, 83, 85, 88
*The Hi-Riders* 23
Hill, Jack 5-6, 7, 40, 65-72
*Hobo with a Shotgun* 4
*Hogan's Heroes* 50
Holden, William 93
*Hollywood Boulevard* 39
*Hollywood Hillside Strangler* 97
*Hollywood Strangler Meets the Skid Row Slasher* 149, 158, 160
*The Holy Mountain* 73, 74, 75, 76
*The Host* 65
*House of Frankenstein 1997* 142
Huff, Richard 129, 130
*Humanoids from the Deep* 37
Hurd, Gale Ann 40-41
*I Married A Strange Person!* 142
Ievens, Edgar 57
*Ilsa: She Wolf of the SS* 43, 50
*The Immoral Mr. Teas* 49, 101, 104
*The Incal* 75
*The Incredibly Strange Creatures...* 149, 150, 151, 154, 160
*Incredibly Strange Films* 3
*The Incredible Two-Headed Transplant* 151
*The Inheritor* 142
*The Invaders* 26
*Invasion from Inner Earth* 121, 127-128
*Invasion of the Body Snatchers* 144
*Ishtar* 91
*It's Alive!* 25, 34
Jean, Barbara 51
Jefferson Jr., Herb 5
*Jimmy the Boy Wonder* 89
Jodorowski, Alejandro 73-77
*Joe Estevez: Wiping Off the Sheen* 7
*Jurassic Park* 89
Kannon, Mike 157, 160
Kaplan, Jonathan 39, 40
Karloff, Boris 65
Karston, Joe 154
Kasem, Casey 151
Kaufman, Lloyd 6, 79-88
Keating, Charles 101-102, 103
Keaton, Buster 79, 150
Kennedy, George 22

*Killer Instinct* 23
Klein, Allen 74
Kline, Helen 124
Korman, Harvey 49
Kotto, Yaphet 25, 27
Kovacs, Laszlo 51
Kyphers, Dale 133
Lancaster, Stuart 52
Landau, Martin 22
Lanza, Anthony 151
*The Las Vegas Serial Killer* 158
*The Las Vegas Thrill Killers* 158
*Las Vegas Weekend* 150
*A League of their Own* 87
Lee, Sheldon 20
*The Lemon Grove Kids Go to Hollywood* 152
*The Lemon Grove Kids Meet the Green Grasshopper* 152
*The Lemon Grove Kids Meet the Monsters* 152, 160
Leone, Sergio 14
Lewis, Herschell Gordon 3, 43, 45, 47, 48, 49, 55, 89-93, 121, 124, 126-127, 134
*Limb to Limb* 141
*Little Caesar* 25, 26, 27
*Little Shop of Horrors* 37, 42
*Living Venus* 49, 91
*Living Things* 141
*Lock, Stock, and Two Smoking Barrels* 34
*Long Swift Sword of Siegfried* 52
Long, Will 160
*Lorna* 101
*Love Camp 7* 43
Lucas, George 146
*Lustful Turk* 52
Lustig, William 95-100
Lyles, A.C. 52
*Machete* 4
*Mad Dog Coll* 23
*Mafia Cop* 161
*The Majorettes* 141
*Make Your Own Damn Movie!* 79
*Making Movies: The Inside Guide to Independent Movie Production* 141
Maltin, Leonard 141
*The Maneater* 51
*Maniac* 95, 96, 97, 98, 100
*Maniac Cop* 6, 95, 99, 100
*The Maniacs Are Loose* 154, 161
*Mansion of the Doomed* 14
*Mark of the Astro-Zombies* 109
Marsh, Sy 27
Martin, D'Urville 31-2
Martin, Dean 27
Maslon, Jimmy 55
Matheson, Richard 41
McQueen, Steve 157
*Mean Streets* 42

Meeker, Ralph 132
Mehoff, Jack 19
Melville, Sam 51
*The Metabarons* 75
Metro-Goldwyn-Mayer 21
Metzger, Radley 51
Meyer, Russ 3, 48, 49, 52, 101-108, 109
*Midnight* 141
*Midnight 2: Sex, Death and Videotape* 142
*Midnight Express* 116
Mikels, Ted V. 3, 109-119
Millay, Bob 131
Miller, Jason 98
*A Minute to Pray, A Second to Die* 14
*Modern Film* 44
*Mom and Dad* 44
*Monster-a-Go-Go* 121, 122, 125-126
Morricone, Ennio 96
*Mothers, Fathers & Lovers* 21
*Mother's Day* 79
*Motor Psycho* 101, 107
Motown Records 33
*Mudhoney* 101
*The Munsters* 151
*My Big Fat Greek Wedding* 6
*Mystery Science Theater 3000* 158
Neumayer, Ingrid 132
*The New Mike Hammer* 23
Nicholson, Jack 42
*Night of the Living Dead* 141, 142-145, 146-147
*The Notorious Daughter of Fanny Hill* 51
*A Nymphoid Barbarian in Dinosaur Hell* 88
Olsen, Astrid 50
*Original Gangstas* 25, 30
*Orgy of the Dead* 109
Page, Betty 52
Palance, Jack 22
Parrish, Leslie 129, 130, 131
Peckinpah, Sam 93
Perry, George 123
Pesce, Frank 95
Pfifer, Frank 123
*Philadelphia* 37
*Phone Booth* 25
*The Piano* 82
*Pirahna* 39
*The Pit and the Pendulum* 41
*Plan 9 from Outer Space* 52
*Playboy* 101
Poe, Edgar Allan 37
*Pocketful of Miracles* 121
*Poor White Trash* 44
*Poultrygeist* 86
*Prehysteria!* 11
*Pretty Woman* 87
Price, Vincent 37
Priest, Pat 151

*The Prime Time* 43, 49
*The Professionals* 152
*Psycho* 61
*The Public Enemy* 26, 27
*Puppet Master* 11, 18
*Q: The Winged Serpent* 26
*The Rainbow Thief* 76
*Rana: The Legend of Shadow Lake* 132-133
*Rat Pfink and Boo Boo* 153, 154, 155, 160
Rausch, Andrew J. 4
Ray, Fred Olen 47
Raynor, Alan 136
*Re-Animator* 11, 15
Rebane, Barbara 130
Rebane, Bill 121-139
Reeling, Robert 137
*Reflections on Blaxploitation* 6, 7
Reich, Wilhelm 75
*Renegade Girls* 114
*Return of the Living Dead* 141, 144, 145
*The Return of the Magnificent Seven* 25
Reynolds, Burt 26
*Ride in the Whirlwind* 37
Ripps, Mike 43
Robins, Herb 157
Robinson, Edward G. 27
Rodriguez, Robert 3, 6
Romero, George 141, 142-145
*The Rookies* 52
Rosenberg, C.A. 98
*Russian Holiday* 23
Russo, John A. 141-147
Ryan, Robert 14
*Santa Claws* 142
*Satan's Cheerleaders* 19, 23
*Satan's Sadists* 19, 20, 21
Savini, Tom 141
Saxon, Vin 156
Sayles, John 41
*Scanners* 132
*Scary Movie* 21
Schwartz, Tom 133
Scorsese, Martin 37, 39, 40, 41-42, 106
*Scorsese on Scorsese* 41
*Scream Queens* 142
Screen Actors Guild 20
*Scum of the Earth* 45
*Seduce and Destroy* 114
*Seduction of the Innocent* 46
*The Selected* 128
*Serial Mom* 89
*The Seven Ups* 97
*Sgt. Kabukiman, NYPD* 79, 81, 84, 88
*Shaft* 27
Shakespeare, William 81
*Sharktopus* 40
Shea, Cindy 154

*Shrek* 90
*Sight Unseen* 22
*The Silence of the Lambs* 37
Sinatra, Frank 27
*Slash of the Knife* 56-57
*Slashed* 160
*Slaughter Party* 79
*Slaughter's Big Rip-Off* 33
*A Smell of Honey, a Swallow of Brine* 51
Smith, Shawnee 6
*Soft Skin on Black Silk* 51
Solomon, Joe 118
Sonney, Lewis 43
*Space Thing* 52
Spielberg, Steven 15
Spinell, Joe 97
*Squeeze Play* 87
*Stagecoach* 145
Stanford, Dok 126
*Star Games* 23
*Star Wars* 146
*Starlet* 52
Steckler, Ray Dennis 149-161
Stone, Oliver 88
*Student Bodies* 21
*The Stuff* 31
*Stuff Stephanie in the Incinerator* 85
*Subhumanoid Meltdown* 83
*Suburban Roulette* 89, 91
*Summer Fun* 158, 161
*Super Vixens* 107
*Superfly* 27
*Surf Nazis Must Die* 87
Swaggart, Jimmy 103
*Switchblade Sisters* 70
Tarantino, Quentin 3, 6, 26, 39, 89
*Targets* 40
*A Taste of Blood* (book) 4
*A Taste of Blood* (film) 89, 91
Taylor, Jackie 20
Taylor, Robert 21
*Teenage Cat Girls in Heat* 88
*Teenage Psycho Meets Bloody Mary* 149, 154, 155
*The Terror* 65
*Terror at Half Day* 121, 122, 123-4, 126-7
*The Texas Chainsaw Massacre* 45, 89, 145
*That Man Bolt* 34
*There's Always Vanilla* 141
Thompson, Peter 124, 126
Thorne, Dyanne 51
*The Thrill Killers* 150, 154, 156, 159, 160, 161
Tiny Tim 136
*Tourist Trap* 14
*Town & Country* 91
Towne, Robert 42
*The Toxic Avenger* 79, 81, 86

*The Toxic Avenger Part IV* 88
*Trader Hornee* 52
*Trancers* 11
Travis, June 124
*Troll* 11
*Troma's War* 85
Tucker, ED 150
*Tusk* 76
*The Twilight Zone* 132
*Twist All Night* 122
*Twist Craze* 121-122
*Twisters Revenge* 138, 139
*Two Thousand Maniacs!* 43, 45, 47-48, 49, 50, 89, 91, 92
*Uncle Sam* 95
*Under Siege* 88
*The Undertaker and His Pals* 46
Universal Pictures 34
Van Hentenryck, Kevin 58
*Variety* 46, 106
Vaughan, Sara 32
*Vegas in Space* 83, 88
*Vigilante* 95-96, 98
*Vixen!* 101, 107, 108
*Voodoo Dawn* 141
*Wacko* 21
Waite, John 161
Walker, Stacey 51
Wallace, Mike 106
*War Cat* 114
Ward, Bill 156
Washington, Denzel 27
Wasserman, Lew 35
Waters, John 89, 109
*Welcome Home Brother Charles* 7
Weng Weng 77
Werner, Peter 142
Wester, Keith A. 153
Wheeler, Edith 20
*Wild Guitar* 151
*Wild Ones on Wheels* 160
*Wild World of Sports* 152
William, Mary Lou 47
Williams, Bill 129
Williamson, Fred 25, 27, 28, 29, 30-31, 32, 34-35
Willis, Bruce 88
*Win, Lose or Die* 90
*Without Warning* 22, 23
Woo, John 46
Woolner, Larry 134
*The Worm Eaters* 109, 117
Wynorski, Jim 47
*Young Actors Guide to Hollywood* 20
Z'Dar, Robert 6
Zanuck, Darryl 103
*Zombiegeddon* 7

www.ingramcontent.com/pod-product-compliance
Lightning Source LLC
Chambersburg PA
CBHW051937160426
43198CB00013B/2191